IDENTITY

Other books by Dr. Wayne Scott Andersen

Dr. A's Habits of Health

Living a Longer Healthier Life

Discover Your Optimal Health

Other books by Robert Fritz

The Path of Least Resistance

Creating

Corporate Tides

The Path of Least Resistance for Managers

Your Life As Art

The Managerial Moment of Truth

Elements – The Writings of Robert Fritz

IDENTITY

ROBERT FRITZ
DR. WAYNE SCOTT ANDERSEN

The quote from Leary Gates on page 23 was used with permission of the author. Quote on page 124 is from *A Mindful Nation* by Tim Ryan (Hay House, 2013).

Printed in the United States

10 9 8 7 6 5 4 3 2 1

ISBN: 978-0-9981862-0-7

Newfane Press
P.O.Box 189
Newfane, Vermont 05345
Email: Seminars@robertfritz.com
Website: www.robertfritz.com
Ordering Information: Seminars@robertfritz.com

PRINTED IN VERMONT ON PAPER WITH PULP THAT COMES FROM FSC-CERTIFIED FORESTS, MANAGED FORESTS THAT GUARANTEE RESPONSIBLE ENVIRONMENTAL, SOCIAL, AND ECONOMIC PRACTICES. MADE WITH A CHLORINE-FREEPROCESS (ECF: ELEMENTAL CHLORINE FREE).

To my wife and colleague Rosalind,
Simply the best...for you, darling!

—Robert

•

This book has the power to redirect our energy on creating
what is most important in our life.
For me it has lead to:

My joy in witnessing Savannah as she has taken wings
and has become an amazing woman.
My excitement watching and being a part of Erica growing up
and really getting what life is all about.
Living a amazingly blessed life and changing the world with my wife
and best friend Lori.
And the time to hang out with my Mom, and so grateful
we can be a bigger part of each others lives.

—Wayne

CONTENTS

IDENTITY

Chapter 1

IDENTITY

AT A CRITICAL MOMENT IN HIS LIFE, the great English actor Alastair Sim came to an almost funny conclusion about himself. He decided he was a fool. In this day of mandatory high self-esteem and "love yourself" mania, this might seem like heresy of the first order; but for Sim, it was a new experience of freedom. He felt like a weight had been lifted off of his shoulders. He suddenly felt energy flowing through him, and, most importantly, he was then able to focus upon what really mattered to him, which was his discipline and art of acting. He said that once he knew he was a fool, he didn't feel the need to be clever. He could be what he thought himself to be: the fool he was. And then he went on to become one of the greatest actors of English theater and film. His most enduring role was that of Ebenezer Scrooge in the most beloved of all versions of *A Christmas Carol.*

The self-esteem movement is about one thing, and one thing only: identity. The theory is rather simple. If you don't think well of yourself, you won't think you deserve success. You would, therefore, somehow sabotage yourself, underachieve, thwart your best efforts, and live a miserable life. If you did have high self-esteem, you would bravely face obstacles, take risks, and be able to leap tall buildings in a single bound. You must, according to the self-esteem movement, think well of yourself, or else you are doomed.

It seems that people in this movement have never read one of the many biographies of successful people. If they had, they would be shocked to learn that the majority of the most successful people in history have had low self-esteem. Mariah Carey said, "I've always had really low self-esteem, and I still do." David Bowie said, "I had enormous self-image problems and very low self-esteem." Bob Dylan said, "All I can do is be me, whoever that is." It's not just successful rock stars who have low self-esteem; so did Einstein, Hemingway, Churchill, Eleanor Roosevelt, Robert Kennedy, Joe DiMaggio, Amelia Earhart, Edison, Elvis, Cary Grant, Alfred Hitchcock, Abraham Lincoln, Mother Teresa, Martin Luther King, Jr., Beethoven, Walt Disney—and the list goes on and on.

Their success was not a factor of identity, but of something more powerful and enduring: the motivation to accomplish the outcomes they wished to create. In other words, they focused upon what they were creating, not upon themselves.

The current overwhelming social agreement about self-esteem has led to public policy and millions of dollars dedicated to self-esteem programs. The California Task Force to Promote Self-Esteem and Personal and Social Responsibility (1990, p. 4) claimed: "Self-esteem is the likeliest candidate for a social vaccine, something that empowers us to live responsibly and that inoculates us against the lures of crime, violence, substance abuse, teen pregnancy, child abuse, chronic welfare dependency, and educational failure. The lack of self-esteem is central to most personal and social ills plaguing our state and nation."

President Dwight D. Eisenhower said, “Always take your job seriously, never yourself.” This is pretty good advice from the man who led the Allies to victory in Europe during WWII. Advice of this nature is easy to understand and hard to take. But why?

Plato’s adage, “know thyself,” has been taken to heart by humanity without question; yet questions of identity have plagued humanity for centuries. This has led to a historic and destructive pattern resulting in prejudice, war, and genocide. On the personal level, it has encouraged a dysfunctional obsession in which people tie everything they do to how it makes them look to themselves and others.

In modern times, an entire industry tells us that what we think about ourselves is the most critical question we can answer in life. Self-help guru Anthony Robbins said, “What we can or cannot do, what we consider possible or impossible, is rarely a function of our true capability. It is more likely a function of our beliefs about who we are.” Rarely a function of our true capability? Tell that to a great musician, or a great surgeon, or a great racecar driver, or a great filmmaker, or a great architect, or a member of any other profession that demands true capability. When one is truly capable, belief in oneself is irrelevant. What *is* relevant is being in touch with reality, which includes a true assessment of one’s capabilities. Moshe Feldenkrais, a physicist and judo master who spent years studying how people learn, said, “Willpower is necessary only where the ability to do is lacking.” To him, the more capable you are, the less you need to convince yourself that you can do something you do not, in fact, have the ability to do.

Here are two strategies you can adopt. One is to try to impose a positive belief upon yourself. The other is to develop your *actual* abilities, capacity, and experience. When we contrast belief vs. ability, ability wins almost all the time, because it is based in reality—not fiction, not faith, not conviction. Belief and ability are not related in that they can exist separately from each other. Here are all of the possibilities:

Positive belief, high abilities
Negative belief, high abilities
Negative belief, low abilities
Positive belief, low abilities.

This last category was made famous in a Stanford University study in which those who thought well of their abilities performed at substandard measurements compared to those who thought their abilities were not very developed. This study demonstrated that belief in themselves gave the test subjects a false and inflated sense of competence, while those who demonstrated a higher level of competence didn't happen to believe in their own abilities.

One of the founders of the positive thinking movement, Norman Vincent Peale, said, "Believe in yourself! Have faith in your abilities! Without a humble but reasonable confidence in your own powers, you cannot be successful or happy." This sounds good on paper, but is contradicted by the history of successful people. Let's look more closely at his assertions, starting with "faith in your abilities." According to many dictionaries, the word *faith* usually means "a belief that is held with a lack of, in spite of, or against reason or evidence." How can you have reasonable confidence in your own powers unless you have reasonable evidence to support such confidence? If you are sane, you will have a lot of trouble doing this. Sanity consists of the ability to be in touch with reality—and this includes your true abilities, track record, capacity to learn, and patterns of success or failure.

Earl Nightingale said, "We become what we think about."

Let's analyze the implications of this statement. The first idea to notice is the phrase "we become." In other words, how we see and understand ourselves will result from the next part of the statement, "what we think about." The further implication: if you want to see yourself as good, positive, productive, creative, and a wonderful human being, you must think thoughts that are consistent with that. God forbid you ever think critically or negatively, or hold opinions that do not reflect how wonderful the world is. Since we can divide the statement into two parts, we can change one of them as a thought experiment—for example, "we become what we eat." So, if you eat a steak, you become a steak. If you eat a chicken, you become a chicken. How about, "we become the way we dress?" If you wear jeans, you become jeans. If you wear an evening dress, you must always be nighttime in the city, just arriving at the party and hoping people notice. "You become the books you've read." If you've read *Gone with the Wind*, you become Rhett or Scarlett or Brandy, or Sherman's March to the Sea. If you've read *Zen and the Art of Motorcycle Maintenance*, you become a motorcycle or a Zen master.

To link identity to anything makes the subject of the link seem important. You are your car, your toothpaste, your education, your heart, your mind, your physical condition, your politics, your astrology, your psychology, etc. Your identity *equals* the subject of the statement. It is easy to see how quickly this false, synthetic relationship becomes silly and absurd. You are the color of your hair, your nose, your eyebrows, your toenails, your moles, your family traditions, your dog, your cat, your kitchen sink.

Of course, these types of positive-thinking "believe-in-yourself" declarations lead people to obsess about their self-opinion as if that were the key to success. Tom Wolfe's description of the "me generation" of the seventies has infiltrated our social structures to the point where it seems as if our main spiritual, psychological, metaphysical, collective, and personal mission in life is to define ourselves. And there is only one type of definition that is acceptable: *narcissistic.* "Love yourself" posters fill the windows of bookstores across the country and beyond. There are over 5000 books on Amazon with titles that include the phrase "love yourself:" *How to Love Yourself, How to Love Yourself: A Guide to Building Self-Esteem, Love Yourself Like Your Life Depends On It, Love Yourself: How to Have More Self-Confidence and How to Be Happy, Love Yourself: The Secret Key to Transforming Your Life, How to Love Yourself: Overcome Social Anxiety and Depression*...and on it goes.

It is hard to determine what came first, the proposition that you must love yourself if you are to be happy, or the explanation that most ills are the product of low self-esteem. Nowadays, the popular view is that failure comes from self-loathing. If you don't love yourself, you will have a bad life. If you do love yourself, you will have a good life. Therefore, you must learn to love yourself. However, if you don't happen to love yourself, all of your disappointments in career or relationships can be tracked to the horrendous root problem of low self-esteem.

You may have bought the party line. The logic of the theory seems compelling enough, and there is a built-in rational for any failure you may have: you just didn't love yourself enough. Often missing in these "love yourself" theories is the relationship between action, competence, strategy, learning patterns, experience, and other direct factors critical to success. If the person didn't get the job, it wasn't because the other candidates were more qualified; it was because she didn't love herself enough. If the person wasn't able to make a go of his marriage, he suffered from low self-esteem. The modern standard of measurement in most things these days is not how well you actually performed, but how well you loved yourself.

Love is Not a Matter of Choice

Here is a basic fact of life. Some people love themselves, and some do not. There is no particular meaning in either position. There are very good people who love themselves, and there are very good people who do not—*but*, and this is a big *but*, nonetheless, *you want good things for yourself.* The degree to which you love yourself is irrelevant.

You could love yourself or hate yourself, or find yourself anywhere on the continuum, yet no matter where you are on the "love scale," you want to be involved with the things that matter most to you. You want to live in ways that are consistent with your most deeply-held values. You want to achieve your aspirations.

Notice that self-love and the desire for a good life are independent factors. They are not related at all. However, the moment they become linked, your understanding of cause and effect are plagued with misconceptions and false impressions. You miss the obvious reality: that you *do* want a good life, no matter what you think of yourself. To prove the point, here is a test question to answer: *do you want a good life*? The answer is *yes* or *no*. Not too many people answer *no*, no matter what they think of themselves.

Have you ever tried to love someone you didn't love? If you've tried, you have seen that it doesn't work, no matter how sincere you are. There are many things in life that are subject to choice. *Love is not one of them.* If we could choose who to love, there would never be unrequited love, because we would only choose to love people who love us back, and all of those great pop and rock songs about unrequited love would never have been written.

The same principle holds true when it comes to loving yourself. You may have thought you needed to love yourself, or you would be a failure. Since you don't want to fail, you may have tried to love yourself—but you were not able to force yourself into it, any more than you can force yourself to love other people you don't love. You may have followed self-help advice by staring at yourself in the mirror, or writing yourself little love notes, or repeating affirmations about how much you love yourself. After all of this, the effort will have proven itself to be futile, because the subtext you are really affirming is this: "I am telling myself I love myself because actually I don't think I do." We can call this the boomerang effect. The intention backfires, and what you think you are asserting is contradicted by asserting it. "I love myself" translates into "I don't love myself."

Issues of Identity

Most people who read this book will have some form of identity issue, because most *people* have an identity issue. Most people are concerned with how they see themselves, or how others see them. This issue may be mild or severe, but if identity is a factor in your life, you limit yourself in what you can create, achieve, learn, experience, reach, and understand. Why? When you are learning, you can look like an awful fool, or terribly inept, or appallingly stupid, or offensively clumsy, or horrendously incompetent. The learning curve usually dictates that you will be dreadful before you can be proficient. After all, you are learning things you don't know how to do. Identity issues are about what you think of yourself, and/or what others think of you. Since, when you are learning, you can look pretty awful, in order to avoid looking awful, you will avoid learning so as to steer clear of those terrible moments. This limits your ability to create some of the most important things you want to have in your life: things that may require developing skills that are not natural, or learning data that is hard to comprehend.

On the other hand, if your focus is on learning, how you happen to see yourself—good, bad, or indifferent—is irrelevant. You have a different and better standard of measurement: *How close am I to where I want to be?*

Our society attempts to address identity issues by promoting such platitudes as: *be brave*, *take risks*, *be positive*, and *tell yourself nice things*. The clichés can go on forever. According to a survey conducted by Columbia University, 85 percent of American parents think it's important to tell their kids that they're smart. Psychologist Carol Dweck and her team from Columbia studied the effect of telling students they were smart. Her research has been seminal. Dweck's team conducted a series of experiments on 400 students in the fifth grade. The children were given an easy puzzle to solve. Students were divided into two groups. One group received praise for their results, and the other group did not. The praise came in the form of only one line: "You must be smart at this." All of the students were to choose a test for the second round: easy or difficult. Of those who were praised for their intelligence, a majority chose the easy test. Over 90% of the other group of students—the ones who were not praised for being smart—chose the more difficult test. The praise represented a disincentive to strive for higher achievement.

Techniques that encourage *undeserved* praise fail to do the job as intended—and, in fact, often do the opposite. The irony is that the more you focus on yourself, the less effective you are. This is exactly the opposite of what modern society tells us these days.

It is hard to consider how wrong and harmful this advice is with an onslaught of maxims from the self-help world telling us that our main job in life is to have a love affair with ourselves. Well-meaning people try to comply, because the logic sounds right. They attempt to construct a world in which they are the star of the show, setting up outrageous expectations for themselves—and then wonder why they did not experience the happiness and satisfaction they were promised.

What has to change? Your basic life-orientation; your focus and the standards you use to measure what is important to you. When you are able to refocus from WHO you are to HOW WELL you are able to create what matters to you, a new world opens. You are in a better position to develop your skills, learn, adjust your actions and strategies, and create the outcomes you want.

Throughout this book, we will demonstrate the structural, mental, psychological, medical, and physiological dimensions of this type of change. This can transform your life. For most of your life, you may have been told that what you think about yourself truly matters, but you will find that it doesn't matter at all. What *does* matter is how effectively you can build the life you want to live.

WHAT YOU SHOULD GET OUT OF THIS CHAPTER

- Forget everything you've heard about self-esteem being an important factor in your life. The most successful people in the world didn't have it.

- You may or may not love yourself, but it's really not your choice. Either way, you want wonderful things for yourself.

- Positive reinforcements backfire. Don't try to cheer yourself up!

- Refocus yourself from WHO you are to HOW WELL you are able to create what you want.

Chapter 2

IDEALS

Do a quick check on yourself.

Which ideals have you adopted for your life?
How do you think you are supposed to be?
How are you supposed to live?
What are you supposed to accomplish?
What are you supposed to think?
How are you supposed to act?

WHEN YOU WERE YOUNG, you may have adopted a number of ideals about how you *should* be, but never been able to live up to those ideals. This is not a personal flaw on your part, but rather the Achilles' heel of ideals themselves. Nonetheless, because you were unable to achieve your ideals, you may have felt as if you let yourself down, failed as a person, didn't live up to your promise, or had something seriously wrong with you.

There will always be a difference between the ideals you hold and how you are in reality. Ideals are abstract *concepts* about how we "*should*" live. Plato called them virtues. Concepts are neither true values nor genuine aspirations. Instead, they are notions, theories, and generalizations of how to live, what to think, what kind of person to be—and perhaps even what kind of work or career to pursue.

The term *ideals* can seem so honorable and admirable, even noble. Yet *ideals* give you a false standard by which to live: one that is inconsistent with your true values and aspirations. Many people confuse the two. Let's be clear about the difference. An ideal is a picture of what you *should* hold dear. Values are what you *do*, in fact, hold dear. Ideals are imposed from the outside; values and aspirations are internally generated. Ideals are a sham; values are authentic.

In fact, there is no particular way you *should* be. This statement stands in sharp contrast to what ideals say. They say there IS a certain way you should be, and if you are not that way, there's something wrong with you.

Here is a common definition for the word *ideal*:

Noun: Ideal
Plural noun: Ideals
A person or thing regarded as perfect. A standard of perfection: a principle to be aimed at.
A standard of perfection;
Synonyms: perfection, paragon, epitome, shining example, ne plus ultra, nonpareil, dream.

Just what are values? People use the term to mean all kinds of things. In fact, there is a precise definition we can use. True *values* come from what you think is more important—and what you think is less important. While ideals are *models* of "good" or "perfect" behavior, values come from our critical choices, especially when they are in conflict with other, competing values. Let's say truth and kindness are two of your values. You go to a concert featuring your sister. Poor thing, she can't carry a tune in a basket. After the concert, you have a conflict between truth and kindness. If kindness were the higher value, you might say, "Sis, you were great!" If truth were the higher value, you might say, "Sis, you were pretty terrible." Your values were not taught to you. This is the popular misunderstanding in our society. They are your own personal invention, something that originates from the choices you make in life. Sometimes, values are thought through, just as you may think things through when you are considering how to spend your time. Sometimes, they are organically generated—for example, when you find yourself automatically supporting one thing over another. Your values are truly your own, based upon what you think is more important and what you think is less important.

Choice vs. Ideals

Many think that if people were left to their own devices, they would get into a lot of trouble: *people are not to be trusted, so we must give them a code for how to live.* This code becomes a system of ethics and morals. You may believe these terms to be interchangeable with values, but they are very different, indeed. Ethics and morals are very much like ideals. They are concepts of what should be important. They are imposed from the outside, perhaps by a religion, legal system, philosophy, or political system. The underlying assumption they have in common is the basic idea that people are not to be trusted—that they need an ethical or moral code to keep them out of trouble. Here's an interesting insight, though: the more your values guide your life, the less you need ethics or morals.

In our experience, people can be trusted when they have the power to choose the kind of life they want to live. In fact, you do want some very good things. You want good relationships, meaningful work, good health, and a productive and successful life. You may not know how to create such a life, but that doesn't prevent you from wanting it. If you *could* have good relationships, meaningful work, and good health, would you take it? Of course you would. This does not represent the adoption of an ideal, but recognition of some of your true aspirations.

Where Do Our Ideals Come From?

For some, our ideals originate with the adults in our lives: parents, teachers, and other authority figures. For others, the inspiration may have been rock stars, athletes, astronauts, actors, actresses, public figures, historical figures…the list goes on.

Think about an ideal you adopted when you were young. You may have thought it was important to live up to this ideal, as if these were secret promises you made to yourself. Then you measured yourself against it. For all these years, in the back of your mind or in the forefront of your consciousness, you had this ideal hanging over you—and, as you got older, it festered there as a built-in judge and jury, saying that you are not living your life the way you should be. You may believe this to be true even if you are tremendously successful and accomplished.

Many people have ideals of what they should have accomplished by the time they reach a certain age. Others hold an ideal of the adventures they should have had. When they do not happen to accomplish or experience their ideals by the deadline, they feel as if they have let themselves down. If you have this going on, step back a minute and review your original assumptions. Why did you think you had to *be*, *do*, *accomplish*, or *experience* any particular benchmark by a certain age? You simply made that up. It is not steeped in reality; it is pure fiction. Yet too often, it seems so real that you become capable of driving yourself a little crazy with it. You may feel a sense of guilt, disappointment, remorse, or shame without knowing exactly why you feel that way. The reason can be found in the ideals you hold—which, by their very nature, cannot ever be accomplished.

In addition, there may be an even bigger dynamic at play. *Some of your most influential ideals are formed by the unwanted, hidden beliefs you have about yourself.*

The Unwanted Belief

Now we get to the major reason why you hold your own particular set of ideals, and it is not because you always wanted to be James Bond or Mother Teresa. It is to contradict a hidden belief: something you believe about yourself that you would not like to know. Perhaps it is something you would hate: something so averse that the belief itself goes underground, hidden from conscious view, neither acknowledged nor understood.

You may hold beliefs about yourself you didn't know you had. Why? Because you think there is something so terrible, so devastatingly bad, that you can't look at it—and to hide this from yourself, you develop an ideal. You did not consciously invent this ideal. It automatically arose to argue against your unwanted hidden belief.

The unwanted belief is pretty easy to locate. Just look

for the opposite of your ideal, and that is probably it. If you thought you were a coward, your ideal would be bravery. If you thought you were stupid, your ideal is to be smart. If you thought you were bad, your ideal is to be a good person. If you believe yourself unworthy, your ideal is to be worthy.

In our era of compulsory high self-esteem, it may be hard for you to entertain the idea that you perhaps hold an unwanted belief that drives your ideals. When you are in any sort of structure like this, it becomes difficult to see the structure you *are* in. First, you need to get out of the structure by gaining greater perspective. When you eventually take a step back, what is going on can become pretty obvious. You may not be able to see your unwanted belief at first exposure, as you've been working for a long time to hide it from yourself—but the ideals you've adopted can be rather evident. What are these ideals? To be smart, successful, useful, good, worthy, purposeful, brave, strong, capable, special, etc.? Why do you need to be any of these things? Who knows what hidden belief lurks just below the ideal? The structure knows!

You'll find below a series of graphic illustrations depicting common unwanted beliefs that generate specific ideals designed to contradict those beliefs.

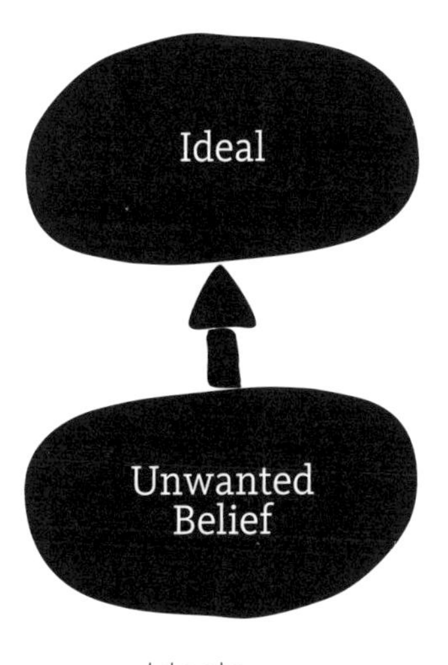

Let's say you thought you were a coward, and that to be cowardly was unacceptable to you. The structure you are in would then generate an ideal that contradicts the offending belief. Most likely, you wouldn't know you had this going on—but you would find any acts of cowardice particularly distasteful, more than most people. And if it happened that you were scared, you would admonish yourself as if you had committed a sin of the first order.

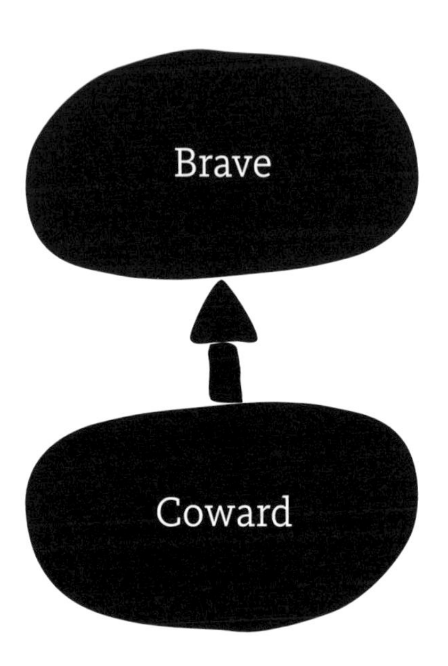

Perhaps you thought you were stupid, and that was the worst thing in the world you could possibly be. Naturally, your ideal would be to be smart.

Everyone is stupid from time to time. Even Einstein was said to lose his keys and wallet, on occasion. Even worse was his dedication to playing the violin. Once, while having the privilege of playing with the great Jascha Heifetz, poor Albert kept making mistakes. Finally, a frustrated Heifetz yelled, "Albert, Albert, what's the matter with you? Can't you count?"

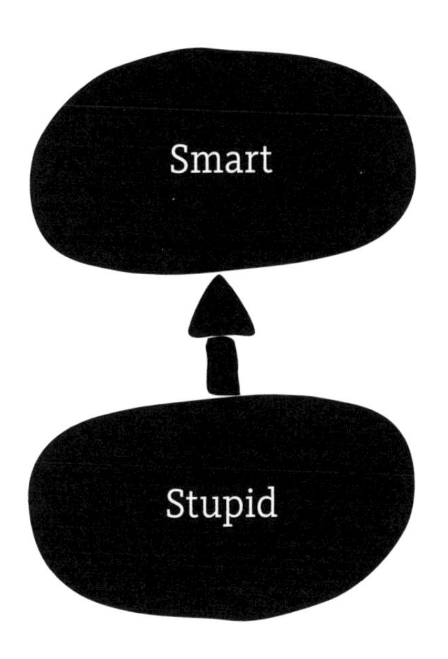

On those occasions when you act like a ninny, if you had this structure going on, you would not believe your sojourn into the land of stupidity to be cute, or surprisingly human. You would find it unforgivable.

The Ideal/Belief/Reality Conflict

There is more going on in this structure than just a single unwanted belief and a single ideal. There is reality: how things *really* are. In reality, the person who holds the ideal of bravery gets scared from time to time; the person who holds the ideal of worthiness has a relaxing day at the beach, which then generates a feeling of not having done enough to deserve such a day; and the person who holds the ideal of being a winner loses. This structure is called the *Ideal/Belief/Reality Conflict.* It is extraordinary how many people live within this structure.

The Ideal/Belief/Reality Conflict generates a strategy, but it is not a product of sitting up nights figuring out how to fool yourself about what you really think. Instead, it develops organically, and all by itself. Therefore, it is a compensating strategy, one whose design exists to contradict your actual true opinion of yourself. The strategy includes two basic tactics: *affirmation* and *experience*. These tactics have a job: to reinforce the ideal and contradict the hidden, unwanted belief.

With affirmation, you have learned to tell yourself that you *are* your ideal. For people who think they are cowards, the affirmation is "I am brave. I am brave!" For people who consider themselves unworthy, it is, "I'm a worthy person. Yes, I am."

Affirmations can be particularly attractive to veterans of the self-help movement. You might find them looking deeply into their own eyes in the bathroom mirror, chanting, "I am a big success. I am a big success." They are trying to program their subconscious minds into thinking they are something they believe they are not. You won't find Warren Buffett standing in his bathroom repeatedly saying, "I'm a big success. I'm a big success," any more than you'd find Cate Blanchett standing in front of her mirror saying, "I'm a great actress. I'm a great actress." In fact, these techniques can create a boomerang effect that we'll explain in a few moments.

The second strategy designed to hide an unwanted belief from oneself is the creation of a *catalog of experiences* that live up to your ideal. If you thought you were a coward, you'd go hang gliding or extreme skiing, jump cliffs on a dirt bike, climb dangerous mountains, swim with sharks, or some other heroic activity. By the way, not everyone who engages in these types of activities has this structure going on. Some people actually love to push themselves, just for the sheer fun of it. This is not so for the person with the unwanted belief of cowardice. He or she needs proof of bravery. There are two audiences for this proof: others in their lives, and the person him- or herself. The proof's purpose is to contradict the unwanted belief, but ironically, it backfires. The need for proof points back to the hidden belief. Who but a person who thought he or she was a coward would need to prove that he or she is brave? The endless list of brave episodes he or she can collect only reinforces what a coward he or she must be.

Often, people who think they are stupid are actually very smart—they just don't think they are. Their compensating strategies may include getting a number of degrees, storing information in their memories so they can tell people obscure facts to impress them, and making smart-ass remarks. They try very hard to prove that they are not the stupid people *they* think they are. Again, not everyone who holds multiple degrees from institutions of higher learning believes him- or herself to be stupid. The motivation tells the story. Have the degrees been attained simply due to innate curiosity and professional interest, or are they meant to symbolize intelligence?

Here's how astrophysicist Leary Gates wrote about it:

> "*Intelligence is hereditary.* How is it that such an innocuous remark has the power to set in motion a profound, life-altering response? Nearly 40 years ago, like many of my peers, I was enduring second semester high-school botany class. I cannot recall the topic that inspired my teacher's comment, nor why a botany teacher would talk about intelligence in the first place. Truth be told, I probably wasn't paying attention. But those three words somehow woke me up.
>
> 'Intelligence is hereditary.' Suddenly, it was as if I was given an important formula. One that would unlock who I was—or, rather, what value I had to offer the

world. I wasn't aware of it at the time, but I grew up with strong messages about the importance of getting an education. This was largely a byproduct of my mother's dissatisfaction with her own life, married to a man who hadn't lived up to her aspirations of wealth and success. Getting a good job came from getting a good education. And getting a good education meant that you were smart. In just three words, all of my old beliefs that education was the path to success were tossed aside. If intelligence is hereditary and being smart is important to success, then I needed to look no further than my lineage to determine my odds of success. That evaluation wasn't encouraging, however. Neither my mother nor father showed any of the classic signs of intelligence. Neither had finished high school. Neither had demonstrated a disposition for reading, except for my mother devouring *The National Enquirer.* And neither engaged in meaningful discourse on current events, apart from their rage at the crooked politicians and the IRS. But I knew from my biology class that sometimes intelligence skips a generation, so I went looking further up the family tree. Not much encouragement there, either. A few brighter bulbs, perhaps, but nothing to give a desperate 17-year-old hope for his future. If I were to be a success, it seemed, it was incumbent on me to defy the laws of genetics and prove my mental mettle. But the solution was hidden to me. I only knew that I was a kid trying to prove that I was smart. So I began carrying around a copy of *Gravitation,* the epic work of the eminent physicists Charles Misner, Kip Thorne, and John Wheeler. It was nowhere near required reading in high school, but everywhere I went, *Gravitation* went with me—all 1,279 pages and six pounds of it. I never read it. Thinking what others might have thought of me had made me feel better about myself, though, and it became a pacifier for my identity all the way up until college. Fueled by my newfound motivation, I abandoned my boyhood interest in aviation and recent nomination to the Air Force Academy for something more cerebral. The Academy's call for 'men to match my mountain' couldn't hold a candle to a weighty course catalog from the University of Colorado promising intellectual freedom. And, so, I set off to pursue my degree in my newly chosen field of study, astrophysics. It has a certain intellectual panache, doesn't it? Only smart people become rocket scientists, after all. That should have settled it for me. But it didn't. My crisis of identity peaked during my junior year of college. I was working on a homework assignment, due the next day, for my Quantum Physics class. It was 3 a.m. and I was in the office at the Laboratory for Atmospheric and Space Physics—an internship I aggressively pursued because of the cool-sounding name of that institution. Somewhere in the sixth page of a Schrödinger equation derivation, it became clear I had severely underestimated the effort needed to complete the assignment. In total exasperation, I dropped my head in my hands and said to myself, out loud, 'I've reached the end of my intelligence.' I was like that guy in the old Comcast commercial, surfing the Internet until a pop-up pronounced: 'You've reached the end of the Internet. You've seen all there is to see.' It sounds comical now, but at the time it was dead serious. I felt defective. And worse: I believed that I lacked the mental equipment to succeed—ever. I was fearful that maybe the formula was right. Intelligence is hereditary, and I had no escape from the shallow end of the gene pool."

•

If a person thinks he is stupid but is actually smart, most people would think, *well, let's prove it to him*. How? Again, by affirmation or experience. Einstein didn't begin each morning in front of his mirror saying to himself, "I'm really smart, I'm really smart." The affirmation route also backfires, and simply reinforces the unwanted belief—again, who but a person who thought he or she was stupid would have to assert that he or she is smart?

An alternative approach would be to take all accomplishments based upon intelligence and use them to argue against the unwanted belief. "Look, you were first in your class, and the valedictorian. You invented revolutionary software that even the best minds couldn't conceive until you did, you won the Nobel prize in math, and *Time* magazine called you the most important genius of our age. Therefore, you must be pretty smart."

Such arguments are perfectly correct. To us, such a person is the genius he or she is *said* to be—but for that person, the unwanted belief doesn't go away. If anything, all of these accomplishments simply reinforce the unwanted belief.

The primal instinct for most people, once they discover that they are in possession of an unwanted belief, is to try to change it or get rid of it. Of course, they don't want to believe what they believe—but how should they go about changing that belief? At the end of the day, only two approaches are available: *affirmation* or *experience of the ideal*. And as we've seen, these approaches can't work, simply because they reinforce the unwanted belief. Let's shift the question from *how to rid ourselves of unwanted beliefs* to *how to better create the life we want,* no matter what we happen to believe about ourselves. The unwanted beliefs we hold are not fact-based, which is why they are so hard to change. If you didn't know how to fly a plane, but then learned how, you would rightfully change your belief from *I'm not a pilot* to *I am a pilot*. Identity beliefs, however, are not based in reality. There is no way to define who or what a person is. Self-opinion functions independently from reality. There is a good chance that the unwanted beliefs you presently hold will never change. They will always be there… but the question is, will they have any influence on your life?

Lady Gaga's Ideal/Reality/Belief Conflict

At the opening of the 2011 HBO production of *Lady Gaga Presents the Monster Ball Tour,* a Madison Square Garden special, Lady Gaga gets a coffee at a neighborhood deli, says hello to some fans on the street, gets back into her limo, is driven past the Madison Square Garden marquee with her name featured in gigantic letters, wipes a tear from her eye, and says *look at that* to herself. Later, in her dressing room, putting on her makeup and looking into the mirror, she beings to cry. "I just sometimes feel like a loser still, you know. I know it's crazy, because we're at the Garden, but I still feel like a f***ing kid in high school." She cries some more, and says "I'm sorry" to the people in the room, her head down.

Well, it's not crazy. It's simply that she is in touch with her real belief about herself—and look at all the evidence to the contrary. At that very moment, she was the hottest thing in show business. She was the highest earner, and her fans and sales were astronomical. She had made some of the best and most interesting music and music videos in years. At that point, she had earned twelve Grammy nominations and five Grammy awards. *Billboard* had named her both 2010 Artist of the Year and the top-selling artist of 2010. She had been included in *Time* magazine's annual *Time 100* list of the most influential people in the world, and *Forbes* had her on its list of the 100 most powerful celebrities. I think we can say that in artistic and professional terms, "loser" is the last word that would come to mind.

But Lady Gaga is not the wonderful character she has created. She is a human being with another name, and a real life. In that real life, she is subject to the same dynamic as every other real person on the planet: she holds an unwanted belief about herself. We can observe that none of her considerable accomplishments have changed that opinion—nor will they. Here's where many people who have signed on for the self-esteem party line will go a little crazy. "What do you mean, she can't change her opinion?" Well, you know the rest of the speech about self-opinion, and how and why we must maintain a favorable opinion of ourselves. Welcome to the modern world.

In reality, *there is no way to decisively define a human being*, whether good, bad, or indifferent. Self-beliefs are not like knowing you live in Omaha because you do—and since they have no possible basis in fact, self-beliefs can reflect only what they are: something you happen to believe, whether the opinion is wanted or unwanted.

So, here was the most successful rock star in years, just about to achieve another example of her brilliant success… crying her eyes out. Self-honesty comes with the territory of being an artist. Most people in this structure can hide an unwanted belief from themselves for long stretches, and only once in a while see it rear its ugly head. An artist—any artist, rich or poor, successful or not—has to delve deeply into the truth of themselves. It takes the deepest truth there is. You have to dig down, right to the core of yourself, and see it all: the bad, the good, and everything in between. Everything is exposed; there is no place to hide or try to make yourself look good. You can't hold onto anything—not dignity, self-respect, or faith. These things are all an illusion in light of what you find. It takes a certain strength—maybe even courage—or you can't get to something *real* in art that nothing else can touch.

So Lady Gaga, her unwanted belief intact, went onstage to perform to a sold-out crowd and blew their socks off—because at the end of the day, what she thought about herself didn't matter a bit to her creative process. Not one bit.

Getting to Know You

One of the principles we will explore is how to get to know what you actually believe about yourself—including the unwanted beliefs. This isn't to change what you believe, but to become *fluent* in these beliefs. One reason you have the ideals you do is to hide unwanted beliefs from yourself. If you know what they are, there is no longer any reason to hide it. It is important that you understand that holding unwanted beliefs does not stop you from creating your highest aspirations and living according to your deepest values. What you think about yourself is irrelevant to your life-building process. We know that this is the opposite of what you've heard your whole life: that somehow, what you think about yourself will determine your destiny. That is simply NOT true. This is a revolution!

The Revolution

We, the authors, realize the implication of what we are describing. At first, most people—especially those in the self-esteem and program-the-subconscious-mind worlds—will be offended by the idea that people can have negative opinions of themselves. That's to be expected. They have never understood the underlying structures in which their clients and followers find themselves. Most often, they are well-meaning; and once they've had the chance to fully understand the dynamics at play, they will have the chance to change their minds. After all, there's nothing like a convert. In fact, several people, some of whom have made their living in the past from leading seminars in self-esteem and positive thinking, have seen firsthand how that approach actually works against the possibility of long-term efficacy in their students. A body of new work looking into the self-esteem movement has concluded that it is not only not helpful, but downright harmful.

Psychologist Albert Ellis has said that the self-esteem movement is essentially self-defeating, and ultimately destructive. He has critiqued the philosophy of self-esteem as unrealistic, illogical, and self- and socially negative—often doing more harm than good. He has pointed out that self-esteem is based upon arbitrary definitions: over-generalized, perfectionistic, grandiose ideals. As a result, he considers the practice irrational and unethical. Psychologist Roy F. Baumeister and journalist John Tierney have observed that the benefits of self-esteem can prove significantly counter-productive, and that parental guidance toward self-esteem may actually thwart practices of self-control.

Psychologist Don Forsyth and his colleagues tested the premise of self-esteem by trying to intervene in a group of poorly-performing students, breaking them down into two groups. One group's poor grades were emailed to them with a practice question. The other group received their test scores and practice questions, but self-esteem-boosting encouragements like "hold your head and your self-esteem high" were also included. The results were unexpected. The participants who were *not* given encouragement did about the same on future tests, but the test scores of those who *were* encouraged with self-esteem support slipped further down. Self-esteem-boosting backfired, leading to more failure.

There are over 114,500 books on self-esteem on Amazon, and most of them try to convince you that shouldn't think what you actually think, or hold the beliefs about yourself that you actually do. Most of them have no idea of the dynamics at play that reveal an annoying fact: there isn't a lot you can do about changing your beliefs about yourself. If you're thinking, "I must be doomed," you are not. The underlying assumption the self-esteem and self-help people make is that what you think about yourself will matter in relationship to your chances of success. Again, we shout: "Have they read no biographies of successful people?"

As Jean M. Twenge wrote in *Generation Me*, "Asian-American young people have the highest academic performance of any ethic group. Asian-American adults have the lowest unemployment rate and the highest median income. Instead of focusing on self-esteem, Asian cultures tend to emphasize hard work—probably the reason their performance is better. This strongly suggests that the modern American idea that self-belief is crucial for success is not correct."

You may not like what you actually think about yourself. In an Ideal/Belief/Reality conflict, because the structure is trying to obscure the unwanted belief, your life inadvertently becomes a struggle between true desire to accomplish the things that matter most to you and trying to live up to the ideal hiding the real belief.

What to Do?

Throughout this book, we will guide you toward a realization that what you think about yourself is irrelevant to your own life-building process; and this change will only be the beginning of a proper foundation for the future, one in which you can master your own personal ability to create the life you want.

Right now, you might have access to the beginnings of this awareness, and that's a good start. There is so much more to come. The great outcome of this transformation is freedom of the sort you many never have experienced before in your life: change that lasts and grows over time, marked by openness, curiosity, and a true desire that is no longer limited by what you might think about yourself.

WHAT YOU SHOULD GET OUT OF THIS CHAPTER

- You have unwanted beliefs.
- These beliefs are so threatening to you that your mind automatically invents an ideal that is the opposite to the unwanted belief, so you can hide it from yourself.
- You attempt to overcome this belief through affirmations or lists of experiences of the ideal.
- In either case, the action backfires and reinforces the unwanted belief, because who but a person who thought they were "that way" would need to prove they were *not* that way?
- Your unwanted belief will not change, because it is not based in reality. BUT, once you refocus upon the outcomes you want to create rather than how it makes you look, what you think about yourself will become irrelevant.
- Don't waste your time trying to convince yourself that you don't think what you actually think.
- It doesn't matter what you think about yourself in your life-building process.
- All of these points should be a revelation, and have the possibility of changing your life!

Chapter 3

WHO ARE YOU?

How do you define yourself? There exist many potential answers—from the toothpaste you use to the car you drive, where you live, how much money you make, how well your kids did in school, your politics, your religion, your profession…and on and on it goes.

At a dinner party, two of the guests were economists. One of them began to make the assertion that the worth of a person was directly tied to how much money he or she made. As it happened, the other economist was an academic who did not make a lot of money himself. In exploring the idea, the first economist became more and more entrenched in his belief that the worth of a human being was directly connected to earning power—inadvertently insulting his academic colleague. His position was, to say the least, extreme—but often, the extreme viewpoint makes it easier to see a concept for what it is.

When a concept is expressed with more subtlcty and nuance, it can be harder to observe, yet the basic thought is the same. To many people, worldly success is the standard by which others—and even they themselves—are to be measured. There is a name for showing off all of your expensive toys to the world: *conspicuous consumption*. This theory was developed by the economist Thorstein Veblen. His idea was that excessive spending by the affluent is motivated primarily by a wish to display wealth and status to others, rather than by enjoyment of the goods or services themselves.

Who are you? Some say it is the most important question you can ever ask yourself. Why is it important at all? The question is truly unanswerable, but if you have to answer it, first ask: "Who wants to know?"

Let's use a little logic for a moment. We cannot BE what we possess. If you HAVE something, you can't BE the thing you HAVE. Who is the YOU who has it? Therefore, anything you HAVE can't be you. You can't *be* your car, good looks, mind, spirit, soul, membership in a political party, citizenship in a country, creed, beliefs, religion, possessions, accomplishments, failures, successes, or bank account.

Think of the ways you may have defined yourself in the past. Were they guided by your accomplishments, failures, education, groups you belonged to, ideas you held, politics, sex appeal, intelligence, moral code, spiritual precepts, or something else? It is easy to fall into the trap of thinking that what you have (or fail to have) somehow defines you.

We often identify people by their professions. A doctor has achieved specific medical knowledge and skill that can be used professionally; a pilot has another set of skills, and knowledge that can be used in the field of aviation. A musician has yet another set of skills and knowledge, as does a taxi driver, a deep-sea diver, a computer repair person, etc.

These types of definitions are based upon facts. There is an objective reality inherent to each of them. However, they cannot define the essence of a person—nor can his or her abilities, knowledge, talents, skills, or professional qualifications. Some professions demand a certain aptitude, innate natural ability, or capacity to learn. We may hold in high regard what it takes to reach the distinguished levels of achievement necessary to qualify for these professions. In reality, these professions fail to answer the question: *Who are you?* You cannot be what you possess. You are not your accomplishments or skills any more than you can "be" your car.

It is easier to describe *what you are not* than to say *who you are*; yet the world is filled with generalized answers that commonly follow a specific worldview. From a spiritual point of view, we could say that you are spirit that has entered into matter; that you are love; or that you are a sinner who needs to be saved. From a psychological point of view, you are your pathology, your hang-ups, your problems, your repressed areas of consciousness, your past traumas, your *gestalt*.

From a communist point of view, you are one of the proletariat (workers); a capitalist (one who exploits the proletariat); or a member of the *bourgeoisie* (tools of the capitalists.) According to Karl Marx, these roles lead to class struggle. Communism, like most *isms*, tries to appeal to identity; adherents are viewed as the good guys, while those who do not follow the party line become the bad guys.

From an Eastern philosophical viewpoint, you are your higher self, obstructed by your illusions and karma. The ideal is as follows: once you reach enlightenment, you will finally know yourself in the ultimate sense—an accomplishment considered impossible until that point. You may have deeply-held beliefs, but you cannot *be* your beliefs any more than you can be your kitchen stove, because, as we said, you cannot be that which you possess.

This leads us to a very useful insight: any way that you might try to define yourself is futile and misleading. You do not have the ability to say what you are; nor does anyone else. There is no right answer to this question, because there is no accurate answer; yet people love to define themselves. It gives them a feeling of place, of belonging, of knowing where they stand in relationship to others. *I'm an Aries with Gemini rising, I'm an obsessive-compulsive, I'm a Type B personality, I'm a vegetarian.* On the one hand, functional definitions such as *pilot* and *doctor* are useful; but these definitions cannot penetrate the deeper essence of who we are. They simply tell us what we do.

Some people claim that we are the sum total of all that we have experienced, learned, thought, done, and known; yet you are the same person you were before you had all of these experiences, before you developed the skills or accumulated the knowledge. If you are working toward building a new career, for example, you were you before embarking upon the career, still you while in the process of learning what you needed to—and, of course, you'll still be you when you become a veteran in your profession.

We can say things about ourselves, but these things do not tell us who we are. We can say what we like and don't like. We can say what we fear and what we love. We can know our values and aspirations. We can describe our good and bad habits. We can care about the people we love. We can hold religions and spiritual beliefs. We can know our history. We can understand many things about ourselves…but we are not the things we know.

In fact, it is good to know things about yourself: your values and aspirations, your patterns, your likes and dislikes, and all of the valuable information in your life-building process—but don't confuse this useful knowledge with the more profound question of who you are.

David Bowie once said about himself, "I didn't try to identify myself or ask myself who I was. The less questioning I did about who I was, the more comfortable I felt. So now I have absolutely no knowledge about myself, and I'm extremely happy." The legendary acting teacher Stella Adler said, "I understood that most people, myself included, (ask)...*who am I, who am I*...until I realized I'm in deep trouble, because I don't know how to do it. I don't know how to find out who I am. This idea tormented me. And I stumbled across an author who finally said: 'Do not try to find who thou art. It is better to know what thee can do, and do it like Hercules.'" (The author she mentioned was Thomas Carlyle.)

Here is the lesson, in a nutshell: *give up the question of who you are*. Free yourself from such existential mysteries. We don't—and can't—know. Don't be fooled by others proposing answers to you. They may be sincere, but they won't be very helpful, given that no one has the answer. These fallacious concepts might make you feel a sense of peace for a moment, but like all nice-sounding untruths, their comfort will run out pretty quickly.

WHAT YOU SHOULD GET OUT OF THIS CHAPTER

- You don't know who you are, and that does not matter in the least.

Chapter 4

INVISIBLE STRUCTURES

MOST PEOPLE HAVE NO IDEA that there are structures at play in their lives that determine how things go. These structures are usually invisible, but they produce recurring patterns. If you step back and look at your life from a greater perspective, you will see that you have two types of patterns: *oscillating* and *advancing*. An oscillating pattern is like a rocking chair. Movement forward eventually leads to movement backward. You work hard to accomplish an important goal, and may actually achieve it; but later in the story, there is a reversal. Somehow, things go in the wrong direction, and you lose the success you created. While the details from story to story may be different, the overall steps in the pattern are the same. The technical term for this phenomenon is called the *macrostructural pattern.*

The other type of pattern—the advancing pattern—has a happier ending. Once you accomplish a successful outcome, that success becomes the platform for future successes. Your success is sustainable, and becomes the foundation for future successes.

We want to help you create an advancing pattern in your life. To accomplish that goal, we need to consider the subject of this book: *identity*. As you continue to read, you will see how identity issues lead to an oscillating pattern in which success is reversed. As we explore various aspects of identity, you will have the chance to move from a self-defeating oscillating pattern to an advancing pattern, the best foundation for your overall well-being and life-building process.

Underlying Structures

The underlying structure of anything will determine its behavior. Think about how you walk through a building. The structure determines the route: how you get from floor to floor, which hallways you need to take, and so on. Think about a car engine. The structure of the engine makes it possible for the car to move from point A to point B. The structure of the road system determines where you can (and should) drive. Think about a supermarket. The layout of the groceries, organized in aisles, determines the course you will take when shopping. Like these physical structures, your life has routes it follows: places that force you to take one direction over another, and sometimes, dead ends, cul-de-sacs, or one-way streets. If you are in an oscillating pattern, no matter how sincere you are, how strong your intention, or how determined, capable, and worthy you may be, the story will go the same way it has always gone: success will not last. There will be a reversal, and, in the end, you will no longer have what you wanted. The business success turned into a business loss; the great relationship didn't last; the project started out well, but then crashed and burned.

You might think it is your fate, or in the stars, or your karma, or your destiny. *It isn't any of those things.* Instead, it is the structure in which you find yourself— because, to repeat the principle, *structure determines behavior.* Here's the good news. If you change the structure, *you will be able to change the pattern.* This chapter will give you some basic insights that will enable you to change your underlying structure—so success actually succeeds, and each success becomes the platform for another.

Patterns

Many people try to change their lives for the better, only to find, after a heroic effort, that things haven't changed at all. They didn't know that they were in an underlying structure that determined how things were going to go. If you didn't understand how the structure worked, you could think you didn't have enough stick-to-it-iveness, that you were incapable, that you held the wrong beliefs, or that you were just unlucky. You may have tried to make up for what you thought was wrong by becoming more steadfast, developing your capabilities, trying to adopt the "right" beliefs, or changing your luck—but none of these things will work. You can't fool Mother Structure.

But you can work with her. A different structure will change your patterns and give you a new lease on life. A new structure is a little like starting over again with a clean sheet: the ability to begin anew no matter what the past has been. So, learning about structure and what it takes to change it is life-changing, indeed.

If you have tried to change a bad habit without changing your underlying structure, you may have found that the bad habit came back. It is easy to take this personally. You may think you did something wrong—or, even worse, that there is something wrong with you. *There isn't!* If we took you out and put someone else in exactly the same structure, that person would maintain exactly the same pattern.

Just to prove the point, let's use this example. Someone is not doing well in a certain position at their company. Everything is tried to help the person perform better, but after a while, that person is replaced by someone new. Within a short time, the new person is performing *exactly* like the previous person, with all of the problems the previous person exhibited. This experience is common everywhere, from the smallest businesses to the largest international corporations.

This serves as a great example to demonstrate how the structure—not the individual him- or herself—determines how things will turn out. If you were the person who was replaced, it might be tempting to take your failure personally, but the fact that anyone in the same position would also fail shows how much it has to do with the structure of the position, and not individual in particular.

It Isn't What We Think It Is

Why do we do what we do? We usually assume it's our DNA, our psychology, our cultural background, our education, our neurology—or perhaps even our astrology or numerology. Yet as the example above demonstrates, there is something much more powerful than our DNA, psychology, and the rest of the list driving the action. The new replacement for the position may have a very different psychological profile, vastly different DNA, and a totally different cultural background and educational experience, but the pattern is the same for whoever fills that role. This shows how the structures we are in act much more powerfully than all of the other factors people think are important.

Here's the way it works: if the structure you are in oscillates and you try to change your life, eventually, you will come back to the same place you started. Think about your life experiences. How often have you set out after something, done whatever it took to create it, and even had it for a while—but later in the story, lost the result you wanted? We all have that story. We also have the story in which we set out after something we want, create it, and arrive at true success. In reality, we have *both* patterns in our lives. The question is, where do you spend most of your time?

One of the most common examples of an oscillating pattern occurs in weight loss. People who are overweight go on diets, lose weight, and reach their goal, but then begin to gain more and more weight until, at the end of the cycle, they end up weighing more than they did before dieting. In fact, the oscillating pattern described in medical literature as recidivism occurs as often as 85% of the time. Popularly known in diet circles as *yo-yo-ing*, this becomes the fate of almost all who do not know that there is a structure at play when they sign up for a diet.

If you back up, you will find that many of the events in your life fall into a consistent pattern. Like a dance, the steps are similar, and lead to a familiar ending. Without a change of structure, you can expect things to turn out in the usual way, following your usual patterns. If yours is an oscillating pattern, success will not last. Eventually, there will be a reversal, taking you away from where you want to be. However, if you change the structure, real and lasting change not only becomes possible, it becomes probable. Success succeeds brilliantly.

Structure

This next bit is a little technical, but please stay with it. This will give you the principles you need to understand, and will help you to have a chance at changing underlying structure, which will then give you the best chance of creating the life you want.

Just what is structure? First, a definition: *structure is a term that refers to* ***a single thing*** *with* ***parts****, and these parts have an impact upon one other.*

Let's break that down. First, we can see that a structure forms a single whole—that is why we say, "structure *is*" rather than, "structure *are*." A structure is a whole that is self-contained. A car is a structure. A building is a structure. A song is a structure. Your body is a structure. A cup is a structure. A chair is a structure.

The next idea addresses parts: within this one thing, there are many other things.

The final idea involves the parts impacting each other. A chair, for example, is a whole thing made up of parts, such as legs, a seat, a back, and other supporting braces. Each of the parts supports other parts. If you took away one of the legs, the behavior of the chair would change from stable to unstable. This stands is an illustration of how, if we change some of the parts, the structure itself changes. Remember the principle: the underlying structure of anything determines its behavior. Take away a leg from the chair, and you can no longer sit on it.

The parts of a car, of course, combine to form a car; but the parts *alone* do not make a car. You could have every part a car needs spread out on the shop floor, but they would still not make up a car; the parts need to be put together in the right way in order to function as a car. A whole structure, therefore, is not just the number of its parts, but the way in which the parts fit together to form a whole. This little lesson in structure will become very important later on, when we talk about changing your personal structures so that you can be more effective in your life-building process.

Tension Seeks Resolution

Here's why structure works the way it does. It is because tension seeks resolution...and by tension, we are not talking about stress, anxiety, or pressure. We are talking about physics. So much of our world depends upon tension-resolution systems to make things work. The muscles in our bodies, for example, tense and relax: some of them tense while simultaneously, others relax.

A plane flies based upon a tension-resolution system called Bernoulli's principle. Tension is created by the difference between the air pressure exerted upon the top and bottom parts of the wing of the plane. This is brought about by the difference between the two air pressure measurements. Nature wants to resolve this tension by making the air pressure the same; and, in order to accomplish this goal, it lifts the enormously heavy plane right up into the air.

This is how NASA describes it:

> "Airplane wings are shaped to make air move faster over the top of the wing. When air moves faster, the pressure

of the air decreases. So the pressure on the top of the wing is less than the pressure on the bottom of the wing. The difference in pressure creates a force on the wing that lifts the wing up into the air."

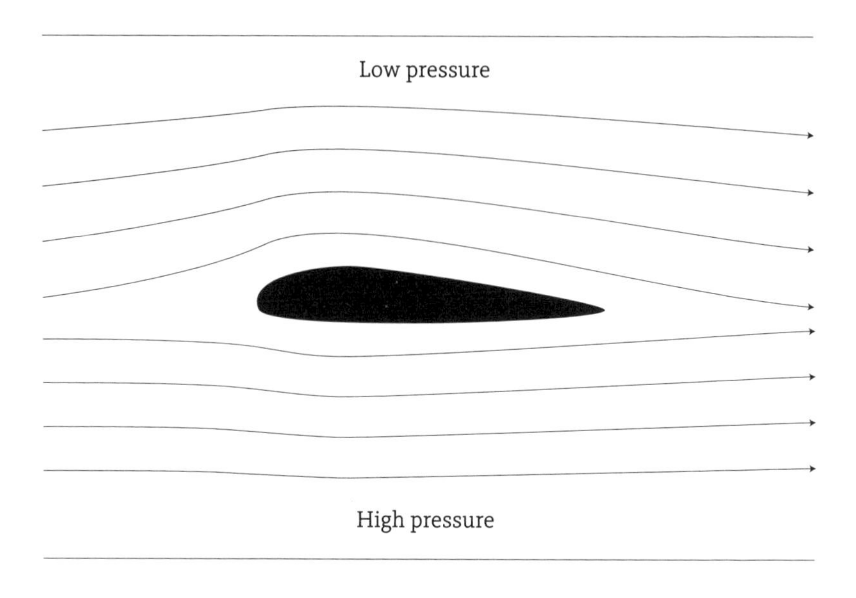

Tension is formed by the *difference* between one thing and another. For example, hunger is a tension formed by the difference between the desired amount of food the body *wants* and the actual amount of food the body *has*. This tension seeks resolution; in other words, an end to the difference, one in which the desired amount of food and the actual amount of food are exactly the same. Actually, to be a bit more scientifically accurate, it is the difference between amount of energy the body needs vs. the amount of energy the body has readily available. That's the tension. Once the body has the required amount of energy, that's the resolution.

Another, more technical way of describing this principle is that structure seeks equilibrium. In other words, within the structure, everything is equal to everything else. Whenever we have a difference, nature wants to end the difference. Hot/cold leads to lukewarm. Left/right leads to center. High/low leads to the middle.

So, tension is like a little engine that creates energy. Both physical forms like planes and the body depend on it. And non-physical forms like literature, poetry, plays, and films, also depend on tension-resolutions systems.

Think of the thousands of films you've ever seen. They have a common form based on tension-resolution systems. Most films have a protagonist (hero/heroine.) This character wants something: to win the Olympic gold, win the heart of a girl, get a job, fight the bad guys, support the good guys. This desire contrasts with what is called the *opposition*: the bad guy, the polluting greedy corporation, the psychopath, the hit man, the evil empire. The hero and the opposition both want the same thing—they both want the girl, the prize, the contract, the credit for the great invention—or they want the opposite thing: the protagonist wants to save the planet, while the opposition wants to destroy it. In film, this is called *dramatic conflict*, which is another way of saying *tension*.

There exist as many plot ideas as there are films. What they have in common is the structural principle of tension seeking resolution. There is the love story form: boy meets girl (and we want to see them together), boy loses girl, usually through some type of misunderstanding. Often, there is another boy in the wings we do NOT want to see with the girl—but for a while, he is worming his way into her heart and creating doubts about his competition. At last, the boy gets the girl back, and they live happily forever. The tension comes into play when they're not together, and we want them to be. Resolution comes about when they are finally together, just like we want them to be.

Alternatively, we could examine the detective story. A crime occurs, but no one seems to know "who done it." Our detective hero attempts to figure it out by following clues. As he gets closer, the bad guys become a threat to him. He outsmarts them and overpowers them, solving the case and putting the bad guys in jail (or maybe into an early grave). Tension: who done the deed? Resolution: the bad guys, who were served justice by our hero.

Take the typical James Bond Film. James is faced with an unbelievably powerful evil organization led by a brilliant criminal mind. Notice that in this type of film, the opposition is always a hundred times stronger than little old James, who, by his wit, courage, and daring, overcomes everything set against him so he can save the world.

The next time you watch a film, ask yourself these basic questions: Who is the hero, and what does he/she want? What is the opposition? What does the opposition want? The answers will give you the dramatic conflict for the film. They will also give you a little lesson in structure.

The reason we are talking about films for a moment is so that you can see how much you already know (but didn't know you knew) about structure. Structure is all around us: in pop culture, rock songs, TV ads, billboards, design, fashion...just about everywhere you look. All of these structures are based upon one principle: *tension seeks resolution.*

Structural Tension

One tension-resolution system we all know about is the bow and arrow. Even if we've never held a bow and arrow in our hands, we know about *Robin Hood*, William Tell, and, for many of us, Marvel Comics' The Arrow. With enough tension on the bow, it can propel the arrow to the target. Without adequate tension, the arrow will fall at your feet. This illustrates the way in which structure leads to actions—which, in turn, enable you to accomplish your goals.

How can we use this principle in our own life-building process? This is one of the most important principles you can ever learn. It is the essence of the creative process, the MOST successful process for accomplishment in history. It has created all of the arts, science, technology, business, invention, exploration and so much more. Imagine using the most successful process in history to enable you to build your life. The best structure to use is *structural tension.* Think of structural tension like our old friend, the archer's bow. With enough tension, the arrow can be propelled to the target, and it becomes easier to act on behalf of your highest aspirations.

The principle of structural tension can sound rather simplistic, but don't be fooled by how easy it is to describe. Structural tension is formed by two elements: *a clear idea of the outcome you want to create* and *a clear idea of where you are now in relation to that outcome* (i.e., where you are now in relation to where you want to be). The contrast between these two points creates a very useful form of tension.

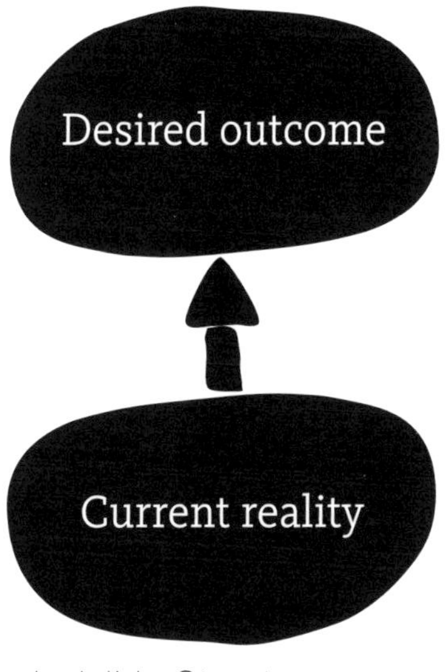

Once we form structural tension, something special happens. Our minds begin to conceive of ways to accomplish the goal. We do this in order to resolve the tension. The mind, like everything else in nature, wants to resolve tension, so when you present it with productive tension based upon the difference between the outcome you want to create and your current reality in relation to your goal, it goes to work. The mind becomes especially creative as it cooks up ideas to bring the current state up to the desired state, definitively ending the difference between the two and resolving the tension.

The mind tends to generate two types of ideas. The first is *convention*: using tried-and-true methods to create the results you want. If you have the resources you need, you can take the types of actions others have taken in order to achieve a similar goal. That's pretty straightforward.

Most of the time, though, you won't have all of the resources you need, and will not be able to employ conventional means. So, the second type of idea is *invention*. When this is the case, new ideas enter your thoughts, and your mind becomes very imaginative, resourceful, and ingenious. It is astonishing how well the mind can find new paths specifically designed to accomplish your goals. *Structural tension* engages the mind to go well past the way in which it normally works.

Once formed, structural tension generates actions, and these actions have a special type of energy to them. Like an arrow leaving a bow as it flies to the target, your actions are well-motivated. Just as the projected arrow has a purpose—hitting the target—your actions have the purpose of helping you to accomplish your goal.

Structural tension is one of the most powerful tools you have at your disposal, but too often, you are unable to use it because of another competing structure we've mentioned. Like a rocking chair, it leads to predictable oscillating patterns in which the success that you first achieve is reversed—and, in the end, you no longer have what you want. This is called *structural conflict.*

Structural Conflict

Have you ever wondered why some of your best efforts didn't always succeed, in the end? Here is the pattern, as we described it earlier. You set out after something you want. You do what it takes to achieve your goal, but later, something happens, and you lose the goal completely. What causes this pattern to occur? The answer is the underlying structure in which you find yourself.

Let's say you are hungry. Again, this is a tension created by the difference between the body's desired amount of food and the actual amount of food you've consumed. To resolve the tension, you eat. When you eat, the desired and actual amounts of food are the same. This is a simple tension-resolution system.

Let's say you are overweight. In this case, there might be another tension-resolution system at play. This tension is caused by the difference between your actual weight and your desired weight. The way most people try to resolve this tension is through dieting. If they are successful, their desired weight and actual weight will be the same, and the tension is resolved. However, these two tension-resolution systems are tied together within the same structure. As you move to resolve one of the two systems, it increases tension on the competing tension-resolution system.

Dieting works counter to the adaptive/survival mechanism of our bodies. We are designed to conserve and store energy, and when we start a diet and restrict our energy intake, or

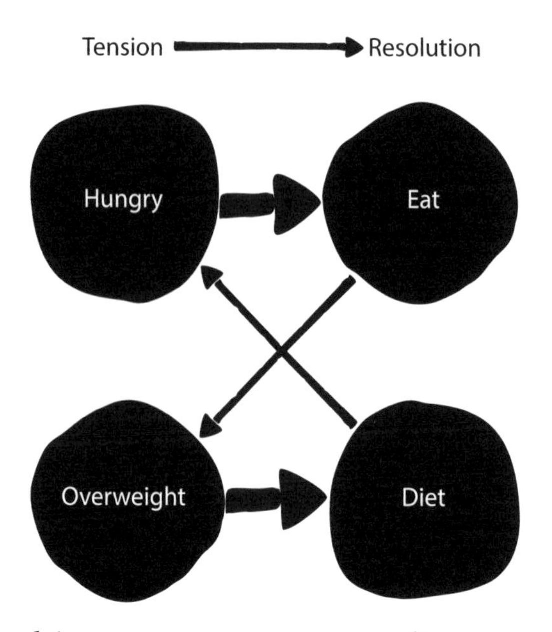

exercise and increase our energy expenditure, we create an imbalance in the steady state of energy. The body, alarmed by the sudden restriction of energy or increase in expenditure, initiates a compensatory process via an elaborate series of neurochemical signals that produce and increase hunger. If the focus is weight loss, the restrictive period will be reliant upon the willpower of the individual to avoid the normal response to increase caloric intake. Willpower, unfortunately, is easily depleted, and is no match for the powerful tension at play in the resolution of hunger—especially in an energy-dense world in which food is always present in every variety, taste, smell, and appealing package possible…and your body is screaming for calories.

Here's a graphic to examine this structure. Imagine that you are at the center of a room. In front of you, on one wall, is the phrase *desired weight*. Behind you, on that wall, is the word *hungry*. Now imagine a rubber band tied to both your waist and the wall in front of you. This represents one tension-resolution system. Now imagine another rubber band tied to the wall behind you, as well as around your waist. The pairing represents two tension-resolution systems.

Watch what happens as you try to reach your desired weight.

You've reached your goal, but while the rubber band in front of you has relaxed, the one behind you—the hunger rubber band—has increased in tension. You are in a structure in which it becomes harder to sustain successful accomplishment of your weight-loss goal. The hungry-eat tension-resolution system is dominant; in other words, it now represents the most powerful force in the structure. Try as you may to hold on, you are up against Mother Structure. And soon, you begin to move in the opposite direction from where you want to be.

Of course, this is the epitome of an oscillating structure. It

is not about lack of willpower, or a negative attitude, or some neurotic urge to drive love away. You are simply in a structure that can only do one thing—and, like a rocking chair, that is to oscillate.

The Ideal/Belief/Reality Conflict

You're back in the room, and in front of you, written on the wall, is your *ideal.* Behind you, written on that wall, is your *unwanted belief.*

Watch what happens as you try to live up to your ideal.

Again, you've reached your goal, but while the rubber band in front of you has relaxed, the one behind you, the *unwanted belief* rubber band, is more tense. The more you live up to your ideal, the more your mind reminds you of your unwanted belief. You are in a structure in which it is hard to sustain your ideal. Try as you may to hold on, you are up against Mother Physics. And soon, you begin to move in the opposite direction from where you want to be.

Now you are beating yourself up with the unwanted belief—but the solution is to live up to the ideal. That is where it is easiest to go, because that is the most pronounced tension in the system. Soon, you will be back to trying to live up to the ideal.

Let's say the *unwanted belief* is that you are a loser. The *ideal* this generates is to be a winner, so you set out to be a winner. You read books like *The Winner Within*, *Dating: Picking (and Being) a Winner*, *The Winner Effect: The Neuroscience of Success and Failure*, or the classic: *The Psychology of Winning*. On Amazon, there are over 19,000 books about winning. These books are especially appealing to those who maintain the unwanted belief that they are losers—and since there are millions of people who hold that belief, many of these books are best-sellers.

The motivation tells the story. Why would you hold the ideal of being a "winner?" This is not the same question as *why do you want to accomplish the things that matter to you*? That question is about creating outcomes, while this one is about identity. In the first question, the focus is upon the accomplishment itself. In the second, the focus is on you—how you see yourself, and how others see you. It is about how you measure up, and your need to stand out, to be special and in control; your need for power and attention; your need to compensate for the belief that you are a loser.

This represents but one example of the general principle. The structure from which you act determines the patterns in your life. When identity is part of the equation, you will be in an oscillating structure, and your success will eventually be reversed.

Let's compare two different structures: one with two rubber bands, and one with only one rubber band. The event is having what you want. An oscillating structure stands as the point of least sustainability, because the other rubber band is always pulling you in the other direction:

"Winners" Are About Identity

Winners take success personally—and they take failure even more personally. Yet to become competent in most things, you need to make lots of mistakes during your learning process. To someone with the ideal of being a winner, failure hurts. It is to be avoided.

Successful businesspeople commonly experience failure as they master their business expertise. To learn, one must fail, on occasion. In Twyla Tharp's wonderful book, *The Creative Habit*, one chapter is entitled *An A in Failure*. In this chapter, she describes how failure is an important component of the mastery of anything. The "A in Failure" reference is about a math professor who encourages his students to fail, on occasion. His idea is that students need to learn to reach beyond their current level of skill and knowledge in order to expand their mathematical creative process. He wants them to focus upon how well they think mathematically, not how they look as math students.

Ironically, our traditional educational system rewards the right answers and rebukes the wrong answers, no matter how much the student learns. This experience gives students the wrong impression: that failure is to be avoided, and that learning is irrelevant. This differs from the approach of traditional education; but in reality, failing and making mistakes represents an essential part of learning and training in the arts. Musicians practice music they can't play yet. Photographers take many pictures to explore their technique. Artists make sketches. Writers write first drafts. True learning includes periods of incompetence as you gain the necessary skills, insights, and experience.

Charles Young, in *Losing: An American Tradition*, said, "I've known I was a total loser since my first college football practice. I've admitted it here publicly, and I am free." One of the points he makes in this piece is that losing is more prevalent than winning. "Football, along with every other major sport, is constructed to create losers. On any given game day, half the teams win and half the teams lose. By the end of the playoffs, exactly one team can be called a winner, while thirty other teams are, literally, losers. So given that 96.7 percent of the players in the NFL can't help but be losers, why should calling somebody a loser be considered such an egregious violation of propriety?"

Well, the answer is rather obvious. Most people take winning or losing personally—as if it said something about them, their character, who they are, or their basic identity. According to Young's description of football's configuration—with only one winning team at the end of the season—winning or losing is not considered to be objective fact, because identity fuses with symbolism, and losing translates into a tragic personal flaw. As George C. Patton said, "Americans love a winner, and will not tolerate a loser." That is how a lot of people feel. Even the terms *winner* and *loser* point to identity, but most demanding professions, such as professional sports, place their focus upon something other than identity. The focus is on learning, improving, growing, and expanding one's capacity to achieve. For this, failure comes with the territory.

> "Show me a player who's afraid to look bad, and I'll show you a player I can beat every day."
> —*Lou Brock*

> "If you are afraid of failure, you don't deserve to be successful!"
> —*Charles Barkley*

Hiding Unwanted Opinions

The natural tendency is to get rid of your unwanted opinions, even when you are unaware of the opinions you hold about yourself. You live in a society that preaches positive thinking and high self-esteem, and seems never to have heard a discouraging word. While your internal tendency may be to hide any unwanted opinions about yourself from yourself, the external environment in which you live bombards you with the message that it is unacceptable to think ill of yourself. If you follow both of these ideas, you will be good and stuck. You won't be able to be open and honest with yourself, and if you begin to explore what you might really think, a whole industry will tell you that you shouldn't. The truth doesn't go away just because you don't like it, but it can go underground, where it can really get in your way. Let the truth be the truth—good, bad, or indifferent. Whatever it is, it is better to know it than to hide it.

What to Do?

The answer to this question constitutes one of the major points of this book. First comes the insight that ***what you think about yourself is irrelevant to your life-building process.***

This insight will infuriate people who make their living in what we call the "belief business." Their idea states that what you believe *will* determine your success or failure. Here are some famous quotes representing the belief business:

"What the mind can conceive and believe, and the heart desire, you can achieve."
—Norman Vincent Peale

"What do I believe that I deserve in this life?"
—Elizabeth Gilbert

"Man is what he believes."
—Anton Chekhov

"It's what you choose to believe that makes you the person you are."
—Karen Marie Moning

"Some things have to be believed to be seen."
—Madeleine L'Engle

"You have to believe. Otherwise, it will never happen."
—Neil Gaiman

If you believe that your beliefs create your reality, you might spend your time and energy trying to manage your beliefs, trying to adopt the "right" beliefs and rid yourself of the "wrong" ones. People in the belief business often espouse the old view of programming the subconscious. They talk about the subconscious mind not knowing the difference between what is real and what is not. They think if you present your subconscious mind with positive images, the subconscious will act as if these images are true, enabling you to move in the direction of these images. *Think nice things, and you will become a nice person. Love yourself, and you will attract love.*

See yourself as a success, and success will fall out of the sky and into your lap—but you must BELIEVE!! To people in the belief business, belief is everything. Introduce this idea to someone with identity issues, and you've got a best-selling book or seminar on how you have to believe that you are totally wonderful and deserving—then you will invoke the "law of attraction," and the universe will send you everything you've ever wanted. It's an attractive proposition: just manage your belief-life, and everything will be just fine.

What people in the belief business don't know is that the structure of anything will determine its behavior. If you are in an oscillating structure, no matter how "positive" and "self-loving" you are, you are going to move back and forth between success and failure. In reality, no matter what you believe, if you change the structure you are in, real and lasting change can happen. That's why understanding this principle is so important to your life-building process.

WHAT YOU SHOULD GET OUT OF THIS CHAPTER

- There exist invisible structures that determine how things will unfold.
- These structures generate two types of patterns: *oscillating* and *advancing*.
- The basic dynamic of structure is that tension seeks resolution.
- Structural tension is the most powerful approach to creating your life.
- Sometimes, a competing tension-resolution system is at play.
- This is called *structural conflict*, and it produces an oscillating pattern.
- Your ideals, in conflict with your unwanted beliefs, will lead to oscillating patterns.
- Once you rid yourself of concerns about identity, you can bring about a change of underlying structure, and move on to an advancing pattern, in which success is sustainable.
- When identity issues are no longer in the structure, you can learn, improve, and achieve.
- The underlying structure of anything determines its behavior, including your life.
- It doesn't matter what you believe.

Chapter 5

POSITIVE THINKING CAN BE HAZARDOUS TO YOUR LIFE-BUILDING PROCESS

Now, there's nothing wrong with being positive, if you are. Yet the technique of positive thinking says you should think positive thoughts, especially when the situation doesn't call for being positive. Books like the classic *Think and Grow Rich* by Napoleon Hill, *The Power of Positive Thinking* by Norman Vincent Peale, and tons of copycats insist that the path to success lies in managing your thoughts and attitudes. The payoff will be happiness, success, and riches beyond all imagination.

It can sound so nice and innocent. What's not so nice is this: *positive thinking is in conflict with most people's deepest values,* which often include truth and honesty. New research increasingly shows the negative side of positive thinking. Social psychologists Gabriele Oettingen and Doris Mayer studied the difference between students who thought positively and those who didn't. They found that over time, the "positive thinkers" put in fewer job applications, got fewer offers, and eventually earned lower salaries. They also found that hip-surgery patients recovered more slowly when they were fixated upon positive images of walking without pain. That is a mind-blowing piece of information—and not something that is well-known in the self-help world.

You Never Want to Be in a Position of Lying to Yourself

Reality is an acquired taste, but once acquired, it's hard to abandon. Reality includes the good, the bad, the ugly, and everything in between. If you had to spin reality with positive, rose-colored glasses, you would go blind—at least when it came to creating the life you want.

You can't build your life on a lie, but that is what advocates of positive thinking would have you do. For one thing, one of the two components of structural tension—the right structure for your life-building process—is your current reality. If you distort current reality, you weaken structural tension. Not only do you need to know what you want to create, you also need to know where you are in the process. You can't portray it as better or worse than it is. That's like saying you're in Grand Rapids on your way to San Francisco when you're really in Kansas City. You can't get where you want to go if you don't have a handle on where you currently are in your journey.

Of course, the people in the belief business mean well. Usually, they are very nice folks who want to support others in creating good lives. Unbeknownst to them, however, the subconscious mind is well aware of the difference between reality and fiction, and if you try to feed it things that are not true, it knows you are lying.

If you claim *I can do it*, is that statement fact, or not? The question is about the *fact* of knowing—not your best guess, the probability of it happening, your hope that it will, or your trust based upon wishful thinking. The term *fact* means *something that truly exists or happens; something that has actual existence.*

When do we know for a *fact* that we can do something? Only once it has been done. We can estimate that an outcome is highly likely to happen. Often, our forecast turns out to be true, but it is only *once* it turns out to be true that it becomes an actual fact.

Your subconscious mind knows the difference between what *might be* in the future and *what is a fact right now*. It is highly probable, for example, that you can cross the street… but if you get hit by a bus on your way to the other side, what was once probable is no longer possible. As it turns out, once hit by the bus, you can't cross the street, after all. When do we know that it is truly a *fact* that you can cross the street? Once you have actually crossed the street, and find yourself on the other side.

While you are proclaiming *I can do it! I can do it!* in good positive-affirmation style, the subconscious is hearing, "I have doubts that I can do it, which is why I need to assert that I can." Not only does your subconscious know *if* you are asserting something that is not a fact, it also knows the *reason* for the positive propaganda, which, ironically, gives it the opposite message than the one intended. *Maybe I can't do it, after all.* Think about all of the people who envisioned walking without pain after hip surgery, recovering more slowly than patients who were not giving themselves positive messages. What "positive" patients were really communicating to their subconscious minds was, *I may have trouble walking without pain*. It's the old boomerang effect.

Those who have tried to practice positive thinking over the years have found that the promise of success wears off very quickly. Of course, the theory is circular for people who advocate positive thinking. The reason it no longer works is because you had a negative thought, and your subconscious mind picked up on that. Now, to be realistic, everyone has negative thoughts from time to time. That's because we don't always like what is going on. It would be a bit weird if you tried to think positive thoughts as a gunman was holding you up, or a careless driver was cutting you off, or if something bad happened to your kids, or even if you got a terrible meal you'd paid a small fortune for.

Many people use the old parking space example to prove the power of positive thinking. They imagine a parking space just where they want to park—usually a place where it is hard to find one. They are connecting their thoughts to their desired outcome, and usually, over time, they come to understand two things:

1. They don't always find the parking space they want; and

2. Other people who have not imagined getting a parking space find desirable parking spaces. In one workshop, for example, a man claimed that the person who held positive thinking about parking spaces was in a better position to find one. The workshop leader asked the other participants, "How many of you have ever found a parking space when you didn't expect one?" Every hand went up.

As we said, you can't build your life on a lie. Positive thinking is hazardous to the health and well-being of your creative process. Users beware.

Here are some quotes from people who are NOT in the belief business:

"Reality is that which, when you stop believing in it, doesn't go away."
—Philip K. Dick

"The good thing about science is that it's true whether or not you believe in it."
—Neil deGrasse Tyson

"A casual stroll through the lunatic asylum shows that faith does not prove anything."
—Friedrich Nietzsche

"A thing is not necessarily true because a man dies for it."
—Oscar Wilde

"Belief is the death of intelligence."
—Robert Anton Wilson

Spiritual Beliefs

When the subject of belief comes up, people sometimes assume that spiritual beliefs are being challenged. This is not the case. Spiritual beliefs are personal, and have their own innate value to a person's life. They are not connected to the creative process, as evidenced by the range of spiritual, religious, and philosophical beliefs successful creators have demonstrated throughout history. Therefore, what you believe on the spiritual level is independent from the creative or life-building process. Spiritual beliefs can be enriching in and of themselves, but when people attempt to make a connection between spiritual beliefs and the capacity to successfully create, they are ignoring the history of accomplished people who did not share the same views. Therefore, it doesn't matter what you believe in relation to your ability to live a good and successful life.

Spiritual beliefs that link to identity are less about what you may think about God, the universe, or faith, and more about *how you see yourself as a believer*. Philosopher and co-director of the Tufts Center for Cognitive Studies, Daniel Dennett, describes a phenomenon that he explains as *belief in belief*. It is not actually a spiritual belief, but rather a focus upon the believer, who is trying to gain personal worth by way of the beliefs he or she holds. To such a person, belief is another factor of identity, an attempt to answer the question *who am I?* Too often, people think they *are* their beliefs, so to rethink a belief feels like a personal challenge—or even an attack on one's identity. Dennett explains that the function of many belief systems is to propagate an adherence to beliefs.

Dennett describes an ant climbing up a blade of grass, falling, climbing up again, falling...and so the cycle continues. He asks, "What benefit is the ant seeking for himself?" As it turns out, there is no biological benefit for the ant. Rather, its brain has been commandeered by a tiny parasite, a lancet fluke (*dicrocelium dendriticum*) that needs to get itself into the stomach of a sheep or cow in order to complete its reproductive cycle. The parasite is driving the ant into position in order to benefit its own offspring—not the ant's. Dennett points out that similar manipulative "hitchhiker" parasites infect many species, all for the benefit of the guest—not the host.

"Does anything like this ever happen with human beings? Yes, indeed," he says. According to Dennett, *concepts* can act like parasites. "The comparison with which I began, between a parasitic worm invading an ant's brain and an idea invading a human brain, probably seems both far-fetched and outrageous. Unlike worms, ideas aren't alive, and don't *invade brains*; they *are created by minds*." He goes on to show how "ideas and parasites have remarkable commonalities, including that ideas are spread from mind to mind, surviving translation between different languages, hitchhiking on songs and icons and statues and rituals, coming together in unlikely combinations in particular people's heads, where they give rise to yet further new 'creations' bearing family resemblances to the ideas that inspired them, but adding new features, new powers as they go." These parasitic ideas have their own agendas, ones that are independent from the health and well-being of the person. The brain becomes obsessed by certain ideas, and their own cause can become more important than that of the individual host. This is why people can act in ways that are counter-instinctive, even putting themselves into dangerous situations, because they are serving the belief rather than their own health and well-being.

A New Pattern in Life

If we could wave a magic wand and suddenly erase all of your identity issues, you would find a new pattern in your life—one in which success and failure lead to eventual future success. Each new success would lay the foundation for the next. Each failure would be the foundation for learning how to better achieve your goals.

The first step in this change is to refocus from identity to your actual aspirations and values in life. In other words, make it about what you truly *want*, not about you and how you see yourself. Once you understand that there is no direct link between your success and how you see yourself, you are free to concentrate upon the subject of your life-building process: how you would like your life to be.

Don't try to manage your beliefs about yourself by adopting a positive image. Avoid trying to cheer yourself up, giving yourself positive pep talks, using positive affirmations, leaving yourself love notes, or trying to control your opinion of yourself. Don't try to guilt-trip yourself into better behavior, or put pressure on yourself in the name of being a better person. Don't spend a moment thinking about what type of person you are. Get the focus off of yourself and onto what is more important—what matters.

Adopting new habits takes getting used to. Old habits are hard to break. At first, this advice will be a little hard to use in your real life; but over time, as you adopt new habits, things can change.

Old habits are best changed by the development of new habits. The new habit is this: if you find yourself thinking about how you fit in, how you look to yourself or others, *shift your focus.* Begin to think in terms of the outcomes you want to create instead of yourself and your identity. You are retraining your mind to focus upon what matters, which is the life you want to create. This new habit can help change your underlying structure to one that supports the successful creation of your goals.

What You Think vs. Reality

Your opinion of yourself, no matter what it is, is not reality. In reality, you think what you think—good, bad, or indifferent. And, unlike factual definitions of yourself, such as "I live in Omaha," there is no basis in fact for your opinion. We could say that whatever beliefs you hold about yourself that are not based in fact are incomplete, and therefore not to be taken seriously. In reality, you may be having a delusion, but the delusion you are having is not reality.

Also, there is no advantage to knowing where you picked up your ideas about yourself, any more than there is an advantage to knowing how you got a cold. The cold doesn't go away simply because you know you got it from hugging your Aunt Jane, who had a cold. What *is* critical is knowing what you actually think—your actual opinion.

If your opinion of yourself is less than positive, most people in your life will not agree—but that doesn't matter. They don't have a vote; nor do you, for that matter. If you did, you would be able to adopt the ideal, and believe it to be true. You are not your beliefs, your ideals, or anything you can say or do—and, the truth is, there isn't anyone who has the wisdom and authority to say who you really are. However, that fact doesn't prevent you from *holding* unwanted beliefs. Better to know your real opinion than try to hide it from yourself for the rest of your life through positive affirmations. This awareness of what you actually think is transformational. It ends the compensating strategy to hide it, which is the driver for the Ideal/Belief/Reality conflict. Knowing your real opinion of yourself can lead to a change of underlying structure with a new, successful pattern.

The Stress Test

In the next chapter, we'll show you how having an Ideal/Belief/Reality conflict generates physiological, emotional, and mental stress that can cause serious negative health consequences in your life. The underlying structure is the conflict between expectation, belief, and accomplishment. Within this structure, no matter how well you perform, how great your accomplishments, or how beautifully others praise you, you cannot reach the ideals you may have set for yourself. The cards are stacked against you. We want to "un-stack" the deck.

WHAT YOU SHOULD GET OUT OF THIS CHAPTER

- Positive thinking is a form of lying to yourself, and weakens your ability to create what you want.
- Your subconscious mind knows that you are lying, and the reason for it.
- Positive thinking actually gives the subconscious mind a subtext that opposes the positive message you are trying to give it.
- Structural tension is based upon two data points: your desired outcome and its current reality.
- If you paint reality with rose-colored positive thinking, you weaken structural tension, and make it harder to create what you want.
- Many new studies have shown how positive thinking backfires.
- If you have unwanted beliefs about yourself, tell yourself the truth about your opinion. This will help change your underlying structure, which is designed to hide these beliefs from you.
- Reality is what it is. Your choice is to see it or distort it.
- Reality is an acquired taste, but once acquired, it is hard to get rid of.
- What you think about yourself is irrelevant in the creative process.

Chapter 6

THE THREAT WITHIN

One of the most important relationships in our lives is the interdependence of our mind and body. You can become consciously aware of this relationship—some of the time. For example, you direct your hand to sign a check; you decide to shout across a noisy room to be heard; you take an extra-deep breath as you dive into the pond.

Most of the time, however, you are more of a casual bystander. Your brain, much like a traffic cop, is directing your body on so many levels, it could make your head spin. It is the control center for your entire body, including your nervous system, endocrine system, immune system, and all of your organs in general. In addition, it must manage all of the essential life-support tasks such as breathing, digestion, renal filtration, and the flow of blood and oxygen to the organs.

The brain takes in everything—both external and internal stimuli—and shares it with all of the other physiological systems that fall under its region of control. When it is functioning optimally, as designed, the brain delivers the miracle of a healthy life over a full range of conditions. It is amazingly resilient.

When a chronic condition or pattern emerges, such as unhealthy eating choices, lack of activity, inadequate sleep, and other detrimental lifestyle conditions, the brain starts to *decompensate* (moves toward the functional deterioration of a previously-working structure or system). And when the control center can no longer do its job, well, the whole system starts to break down.

It gets worse. The biggest threat to the system is not external factors, like bad food, insufficient activity, or a lumpy mattress—things that are relatively easy to address. The major threat to the system is chronic stress. *Chronic* means constant, habitual, entrenched. This type of stress is there all the time, and never goes away. It is relentless. Nothing comes close to the insidious effect of chronic stress on the human mind and body. It is the silent killer.

Your boss gives you an unexpected deadline; your teenager is late coming home from her first date in a car driven by her boyfriend, who just got his license a week ago; an over-demanding client makes a comment that insults your intelligence and professionalism. You feel that sudden surge of pounding and flushing, along with a queasy stomach and emotions that scream *something is not quite right*. This is the same response you would have had 10,000 years ago, when the saber-toothed tiger jumped out of the brush to attack. These moments of stress were needed to survive. This type of stress is situational, temporary, and tolerable. In fact, it is the reason you are here today.

Congratulations! Because your forefathers' ability to respond to stressful situations allowed them to stay alive, breed, and raise offspring, you are here. Your ancestors mastered the stress response as an important aspect of the survival of the species. Without it, we would have a world populated by fantastic saber-toothed tigers.

The brain has two areas vital to producing the lightning-quick responses that were necessary to survive in a very dangerous ancient world. First, a seahorse-shaped structure near the base of the brain, called the *hippocampus*, determined the magnitude of the threat. A saber-toothed tiger certainly qualified as a real threat, and the hippocampus fired off a warning to the *amygdala*, an almond-shaped group of nuclei in the midbrain, to send out a burst of chemicals, hormones, and nerve impulses that told your great-great-great-grandfather to get the hell out of Dodge.

The stress-response mechanism played a critical role in our daily survival, and it is why the human species is here today. It still serves us well, on occasion: for example, when a deer runs out into the road in front of you, and you instantly respond, avoiding a dangerous collision. We've all heard of instances in which an ordinary person generated superhuman power in order to free a trapped child from a collapsed building, for example.

Good as it may be in situations of sudden danger, the stress response mechanism was *not* designed to be activated 24 hours a day, seven days a week, 52 weeks a year, year after year. It is meant to be used when your life is at risk, on rare occasions; not as an ongoing, internal cold war, a condition that strains the system to the point at which stress itself becomes the danger.

When you have an Ideal/Belief/Reality conflict, you have unknowingly signed up for perilous chronic stress. After years of constant stress, your life can be at risk.

Hans Selye, who coined the word *stress* back in 1936, defined it as the "non-specific response of the body to any demand for change." After several experiments on animals, he concluded that persistent stress over time resulted in the very same illnesses human beings develop: hypertension, strokes, heart attacks, ulcers, etc. This finding was revolutionary, because scientists previously believed that illnesses were caused by pathogens (germs). That stress *itself* could be the culprit was a landmark discovery.

In countless stress studies, psychological distress led to physical illness. The brain, which normally directs mental activity very well, becomes overloaded by constant perceived threats to it safety. The threats need not be interpreted as sudden danger or hazardous events. A more subtle, ongoing existential threat is formed by the ideal (the way one is "supposed" to be) vs. the unwanted belief (the way the person thinks he or she actually is). In the ongoing condition, you are supposed to be something you can never achieve; and in any part of the continuum of the oscillating pattern (between acting more like the ideal or more like the belief), the stress is unremitting.

The body has a homeostatic (or balancing) process specifically designed to fight such challenges. This process is called *allostasis*: the mind/brain and body's ability to achieve stability through (and despite) change. This dynamic process is critical for your survival. Any threat or change triggers an allostatic stabilizing response. Like a teeter-totter, the allostatic process is in constant motion, responding to change and threat. This occurs whether the changes and threats are real or not, and whether you are consciously aware of them or not.

The key areas affected are the hypothalamus, the pituitary gland, and the adrenal glands. And when this constant level of stress occurs, the body initially compensates for it with an outpouring of adrenaline, cortisol, and other stress-related hormones, trying to restore the biological system to a state of equilibrium; but eventually, the brain and the body are depleted of their reserves, and succumb to the cumulative effects of a continual bombardment of these hormones. The consequences are first exhaustion, then disease.

The cycle usually starts with fatigue—wondering why you are so tired all the time, and taking a trip to the doctor to get a shot to get your energy up. All the while, your Ideal/Belief/Reality conflict—perhaps made worse by bad lifestyle habits—is escalating the situation. Things spiral to a crisis point, and the body gets more and more worn out. Then conditions like acid peptic disease, alcoholism, asthma, tension headaches, hypertension, insomnia, irritable bowel syndrome, ischemic heart disease, anxiety, depression, psychoneuroses, sexual dysfunction, and even skin diseases begin to emerge, and your heath decays. If these weren't bad enough, the immune system becomes impaired, leading to virally-associated disorders ranging from the common cold and herpes to what some call chronic fatigue syndrome. Scientist are now observing the relationship between the immune-dampening effects of chronic stress, as in the case of virally-influenced cancers like *adenocarcinomas* or *hepatocarcinomas.*

With all we've said, you may be thinking, "What does this have to do with an individual living with an identity issue? Aren't we talking about the impact of a bad lifestyle?" That is only one obvious dimension—one that can be understood, diagnosed, and treated by changing from bad habits to healthy ones. What is not obvious is the underlying stress caused by ongoing conflict between an ideal and its corresponding belief. Even new, healthy lifestyle choices do not interrupt the chronic stress from an Ideal/Belief/Reality conflict.

Unlike situational stress, for which you can *remove* the stressors, in stress-induced by identity issues, there is no way out. It permeates your entire life, and you may not be conscious that it's there. Every day, every hour, every minute…it is there. It may have gone dark several years ago. In other words, it remains below your conscious level of awareness, and is operating on the subconscious level. While your Ideal/Belief/Reality conflict has gone underground, your brain reacts as if it were a real-world threat. The brain thinks it is up against an adversary; it thinks it sees a saber-toothed tiger.

So, if you have the unwanted belief that you are stupid, and the corresponding ideal is intelligence, and you've done a dumb thing...your brain reacts exactly as it would in a moment of serious physical threat, firing out potent neurotransmitters and cortisol to allow you to run from (or fight) this threat to your health. The way to think about this is that there is an ongoing level of chronic stress, and an event that triggers the emergency reaction in the brain. This represents stress upon stress, multiplying the condition. Another dimension is that the immediate stressful situation reinforces the unwanted belief, and adds to the chronic stress by making it seem even more important that you live up to your ideal.

The difference between a real physical threat and this type of chronic stress can be seen in the following example. As you swim away from the attacking crocodile at a speed that would impress even Michael Phelps, your body burns off these stress chemicals, and then you quickly return to a calm, collected state. This is how your body was designed to work. When you are entrenched in an Ideal/Belief/Reality conflict, however, the chemicals do not burn away as they would in situations of real danger. Instead, they continue to circulate in your body, raising daily havoc as you feel a degree of constant danger and pressure, no matter what is going on in your life. Some days are filled with stressful events, and some days seem more relaxed. The whole time, your mind is reacting to the conflict between your unwanted belief, its compensating ideal, and reality as it is. Since your belief is not only unwanted but unacceptable, the continual message is: *you are not the way you should be, here's how you should be*, and *you can't really be that way, because you aren't that way and never will be.*

We hope you get the image of this constant level of stress that exists at all times, even when everything appears externally calm and relaxed. It is as if you were holding onto the chair you were sitting in—as if, if you didn't hold onto it very tightly, you would float up and hit your head on the ceiling. To make matters worse, events take place in which your belief is reinforced and your ideal contradicted. Then, as we've said, even more stress is generated, and it does not burn off the biochemistry as it would in a physically-triggered situation.

A coworker questioning your reasoning on a project at a staff meeting hits you between the eyes with his logic, and you literally cannot see straight. If you think you are incapable and try to uphold an ideal of being capable, this hurts. As you sit there fuming as a result of your capabilities being questioned, the same chemicals are flowing through your veins and arteries as if you really were in physical danger—but instead of being used as they were intended, to create physical acceleration to fight or flight, they are attacking your vessels, raising your blood pressure, and eroding the very organs they were meant to protect. Revving up every time someone threatens your ideal is much like bringing out all of the fire engines for a five–alarm fire. Even though it turns out to be a false alarm, after one of these events, the stress level remains high because of the constant pressure to live up to your ideal, and avoid being like your unwanted belief. This incessant, systemic thinking is in charge, and you continually suffer, both mentally and physically.

The Autonomic Nervous System

In this next section, we will describe nature's design for automatic control of how you interact with the world. Later, we will contrast that with what happens when identity issues are built into the structure.

The automatic control of your vital interactions is divided into sympathetic and parasympathetic components. *In an optimally healthy individual,* in our natural state, we are run by our parasympathetic nervous system, which produces a calm, alert physiological state that protects us and allows us to cooperate and care for each other. The *vagus* nerve is the quarterback, sending signals to our eyes and head to posture friendliness, and to slow our heart and help with digestion and immune responses. The vagus nerve also slows our breathing, so we can take deep, centering breaths. It allows us to be highly aware, fully present, and focused, yet at the same time compassionate and social.

The counterpart of the autonomic nervous system is the sympathetic nervous system. It is in charge of fight-or-flight emergencies as well as the stress response that unleashes supercharged effects on the infrequent occasions we need drastic responses, as described above. Unlike 10,000 years ago, when the parasympathetic nervous system was our natural default, in our chaotic modern life, the sympathetic nervous system is the current operating system. And the news gets worse. The fact is, general stress levels are going up, not down. The American Psychological Association stated that 42% of Americans reported that their stress levels had increased over the past year. The healthy, default state of our parasympathetic nervous system is in jeopardy—and, with it, our health. From chronic stress, inflammation runs amok, turning the foot soldiers of your immune system against you. They attack your vessels, putting you at higher risk for heart disease, asthma, obesity, diabetes, gastrointestinal problems such as acid reflux and IBS, headaches, and even erectile dysfunction. Stress can actually lead to depletion of our memory capacity, emotional disturbances, and even reasoning failure. It has been implicated in Alzheimer's disease, depression, anxiety, accelerated aging, and even premature death.

This chronic state may express itself as an angry, agitated *fight* state with exaggerated emotions. Alternatively, you may withdraw or feel depressed in the *flight* phase. In this state, you have very little energy and may feel spaced out, with little motivation to change your life. You may be paralyzed on the surface, and, simultaneously, extremely anxious internally.

A Change of Underlying Structure

Remember, the underlying structure of the Ideal/Belief/Reality conflict comes from the relationship between two competing tension-resolution systems. One comes from your actual desires, including your highest aspirations and deepest values. The competing tension-resolution system is formed by the rejection of a fundamental unwanted belief—and an ideal designed to hide that belief, which creates an image of how the person feels they have to be. As we saw, when you move toward resolution of one side of the two competing systems, it increases tension in the other system; remember the two rubber bands. But what happens when you cut one of the rubber bands? In more than 30 years of experience with this principle, we have witnessed the most common experience of people who "cut the rubber band." Typically, it is the feeling of a weight being lifted off the person's shoulders, energy flowing through his or her body, a physical and mental lightness, a sense of profound freedom, and a change of basic life motivation. How does this happen?

Imagine that you are no longer trying to be something you cannot be. Imagine that you become fluent in your own beliefs about yourself, whatever they are. Imagine that what you think about yourself—good, bad, or indifferent—doesn't matter a bit in your life-building process. It's like letting go of the chair you were holding onto for dear life. The strain is gone, the pressure is off, the body and mind can relax and return to their most natural state of being. Most people who have had this experience report that they didn't know how much stress they were experiencing throughout their lives. It is as if there had been a loud noise in the room that you didn't notice until it stopped, and you could finally hear the silence.

WHAT YOU SHOULD GET OUT OF THIS CHAPTER

- There are two types of stress: *acute* and *chronic.*

- An *acute* stress-response mechanism enables us to react to danger quickly. This system generates certain hormones, which are utilized over a short period of time, as they are consumed by you physically fighting or fleeing; the body then returns to biochemical balance.

- A *chronic* stress condition that overwhelms the body's ability to restore equilibrium leads to long-term dysregulation of *allostasis,* in that it promotes maladaptive "wear and tear" on the body and brain, resulting in progressive damage to organs, systems, and overall health.

- An Ideal/Belief/Reality conflict generates chronic stress through the continual pressure of trying to live up to an impossible ideal while simultaneously concealing an unwanted belief.
- Chronic stress can lead to diseases, ill health, and a host of related physical problems.
- A change of underlying structure generates a resolution of chronic stress, and gives a person a new lease on life.

Chapter 7

TALENT AND PERFECTION: A BASIC MISUNDERSTANDING

PERHAPS YOU HAVE ADOPTED THE GOAL of *perfection* without even knowing that you've done it. Numerous religions and philosophies concern themselves with moving people from an imperfect to a perfect state, but is perfection a worthy life goal? What is a perfect human being?

Think of it from the identity point of view: that if you are imperfect, there is something wrong with *you*. The ideal of perfection stands as a constant reminder of how imperfect you are. No matter how nice a day you've had, or how great the dinner party, or how wonderful the concert, or how pleasant the visit from friends, or how beautiful the sunset, or how sweet the children's play, or how perfect the moment, there is always something wrong—and that something is called *your imperfection*. A drive for perfection leads to a profound lack of appreciation for life as it *actually is*, with all of its complexities, flaws, warts, ironies, and imperfections.

The Illusion of Perfection

Richard Bach stated a typical New Age notion: "There is such a thing as perfection . . . and our purpose for living is to find that perfection and show it forth..."

Is that really our purpose for living? Many people have adopted this concept without question. What are the built-in assumptions that need to be questioned? For one, we have a job in life, and that job is to be *better* than we are. It reminds us of what Lucy said to Charlie Brown when he told her that we are here to help others. "What are the others here for?" she asked. Another assumption states that our life purpose is to become perfect.

People come by the goal of perfection honestly. It was with us well before the ancient Greeks first invented their Western notion of perfection. Plato, among other Greek philosophers, thought perfection was life's highest goal. He wrote that to reach perfection, one had to transcend the imperfection of reality and strive for a perfect state in which such things as beauty, justice, or goodness are in an ideal or complete condition. Plato thought philosophers had the job of contemplating the nature of the "good," and, in doing so, perfecting themselves.

Before the ancient Greeks, Eastern religions saw perfection as their primary spiritual goal. In their traditions and teachings, perfection meant to make the "soul the real master of oneself," to be above the senses, passions, and worldly concerns. By overcoming ignorance and ego, one can reach "enlightenment," which is seen as a perfect state of being, knowledge, and understanding. This is such a hard job that it takes many lifetimes to accomplish. Through a series of reincarnations, the soul has the chance to become better and better, until it finally reaches perfection. When this occurs, the soul no longer needs to reincarnate, and is free.

The Perfection Thing

We need to make a distinction between wanting to become better at a skill—becoming a better golfer, a better listener, better at personal interactions, a better musician, a better computer programmer, etc.—and *becoming a better human being*. To show how separable these two concepts are, we can see that becoming a better driver, or a better chef, or a better pool player does not make you a better human being. You would be the same human being, with a different skill set.

Why do we think perfection is a higher state of being than imperfection? It is the flaw in the crystal than makes the crystal more interesting. Beethoven's *Fifth Symphony* is, formally, a perfect work; yet his *Ninth Symphony* is imperfect from a formal point of view. Yet, while the Fifth is magnificent, the Ninth reaches expressive heights the Fifth could not approach.

We have seen very nice people ignore the beauty of their lives because of their obsession with the concept of personal perfection. Sad for them, on two fronts. The first is the utter impossibility of defining what a perfect human being is. Even the saints were not perfect, yet they were able to rise above their imperfections. That means they were imperfect, and acted accordingly. So, for those of you who are convinced that perfection should be your goal in life—newsflash—you've come to the wrong planet. Sorry. This is Earth. As Robert Frost said, "Earth's the right place for love. I don't know where it's likely to go better." It is not a plane of perfection, or even a plane capable of reaching perfection—but then, it is better than perfection. It is life lived within the realm of all of the fantastic imperfections of irony, love, and even loss.

When you try to make *more* of something than it is, you deny what it is. Any glorification diminishes that which is being glorified.

When you try to make life more than it is by giving it the goal of perfection, you are unable to appreciate the miracle right before your eyes.

While in many philosophies and religions, perfection is the ultimate goal, in the arts, perfection is seen as a counterfeit goal unworthy of art. Perfection is seen as inauthentic, inane, superficial, and ridiculous. How different it is in the arts and sports than in philosophy.

Eugene Delacroix, said, "An artist who aims at perfection in everything achieves it in nothing."

Hannah Arendt said, "In order to go on living, one must try to escape the death involved in perfectionism."

John Wooden said, "We are all imperfect."

Harriet B. Braiker said, "Striving for excellence motivates you; striving for perfection is demoralizing."

Robert Browning said, "Faultless to a fault."

Beyoncé said, "If everything was perfect, you would never learn, and you would never grow."

Alexander Calder said, "To an engineer, *good enough* means perfect. With an artist, there's no such thing as perfect."

And Leonard Cohen wrote, "Ring the bells that still can ring / Forget your perfect offering / There is a crack in everything / That's how the light gets in."

In aesthetics, there exists a value called *significant roughness.* In other words, perfection takes the soul out of art. There needs to be a little funk.

"It don't mean a thing if it ain't got that swing."
— **Duke Ellington and Irving Mills**

Perfectionism kills the human spirit that art so depends upon. It kills the human spirit that your life so depends upon.

In a now-famous story, told in Robert Frost's poem *New Hampshire*, poet Amy Lowell said that she had given up her summer place in Dublin, N.H. Quoting Emerson, she said, "The God who made New Hampshire taunted the lofty land with little men." She went on to say that she couldn't stand the people there.

Frost answered, "For art's sake, one could almost wish them worse, rather than better." And in that line, Frost expresses a vastly different purpose than perfection—and that is the appreciation of the human condition, as imperfect as it is.

If you are like many people who have a "perfect thing," the best thing you can do is to *give it up.* It is not a worthy goal. It is not really progress of any kind. It is an empty ideal with the subtext of constant self-condemnation. All the "perfect thing" does is give you the impression that you are not good enough, and that you are unacceptable as you are. Why can't you be just like you are? Why do you have to be "better" than you are? Who sets up these phony standards of measurement? What Frost might say is that you are not bad enough for art.

We love our children with all of their little imperfections. We wouldn't trade their little imperfections for what might be thought of as a perfect child. If it is true for them, then it must be true for you, as well.

The ideal of perfection, like all ideals, is synthetic and artificial—and, if you happen to have an Ideal/Belief/Reality conflict in which the unwanted belief is that there is something wrong with you, you may have unwittingly taken on the notion that you need to perfect yourself. Of course you would think that. Your life has been filled with a compensating strategy that exists to make up for your unwanted belief. Notice that your approach has been a dead end. Whatever improvements you think you have made, the structure is still in place, and there is no sense of progress or relief from the curse of imperfection.

Notice if you have what we are calling a "perfect thing;" then begin to explore the cause of this. Which imperfection do you find unacceptable in yourself? Become fluent in your own opinions about yourself. Don't try to change your opinions, but know they are there. These opinions will never stop you from wanting good things for yourself, such as good health, good finances, good relationships, good ways to spend your time, productive work, meaningful aspirations, and good values.

The Talent Thing

One of Aristotle's most important ideas was that whenever there is potential in anything, it will strive to fulfill itself. Later, St. Thomas Aquinas, who was deeply influenced by Aristotle, concluded that the fulfillment of potential should be one of

Christianity's highest goals. Aquinas translated Aristotle's principle into this concept: we contain certain potentials, and therefore, we have our own unique purpose—that of reaching our full expression and a perfect realization of what might be possible. For Aristotle, it was about physics. A seed contained the potential to grow into a flower. To Aquinas, that same principle expanded further to address the human condition: the seeds of possibilities we have within us strive to be developed. Your gifts need to reach their full potential.

Let's take a moment to explore the underlying assumption of this concept. Your gifts, talents, and natural abilities are your potential; and potential, according to Aquinas, has a built-in dynamic: that of striving to be fulfilled. If you possess certain gifts, such as talent or great intelligence or mechanical ability or mathematical aptitude, are you obliged to fulfill these attributes? Does the very existence of aptitude form your life direction, mandating an ordained life purpose in which there is no free choice? Are less-gifted people freer than you to live the life they want? Who decides which of your gifts you are obligated to fulfill? To carry the thought further, wouldn't it be better to have no particular gifts at all, so you could decide for yourself how you wanted to live your life?

If you have the talent to become a barber, do you have to spend your life cutting hair? If you are good at math, do you need to become a mathematician, scientist, or engineer? If you excel at playing the piano, do you need to become a professional musician? To what degree are you required to forge a life based upon your natural talents? To what degree must your talents govern your destiny? People often say, "You have to live up to your talents. You have to honor your talents. These are God's gifts, and they were given to you for a reason." This implies that you must develop them, or risk letting God down.

> "When I stand before God at the end of my life, I would hope that I would not have a single bit of talent left, and could say, 'I used everything you gave me.'"
> —*Erma Bombeck*

This is a common view—that you have to "use up" your talents and abilities. Did God give us free will so that we could use our gifts as we see fit, or did He burden us with talent that we must use? Where is the place for freedom of choice? Bombeck's quote implies that she *must* use every bit of talent she has; before God, she would take pride that she had done a good job with it. Therefore, the implication is that it is not her free choice whether to use her talent or not. The talents determine her job in life, and she has no freedom of choice in the matter.

Identity and Talent

Many people define themselves by their talents. They think they *are* their talents and abilities. If you had this going on, you would pressure yourself to live up to your gifts. If you didn't, you would feel as if you had let God, yourself, or the universe down. Developing them would automatically become your life purpose.

Schools give their students aptitude tests designed to measure their abilities. Then, guidance counselors sit down with these students and give them advice, which usually involves pursuing a career based upon their aptitude. Students who are good at math should become engineers; if they are organized, they should become managers; if they are artistically talented, they should become graphic artists; if they are good at communication, they should become journalists. Many, following their guidance counselor's advice, find themselves in careers they never cared about—and, once they get to middle age, they are ready for their midlife crisis. They know there must be more to life than they have experienced, but they are unable to reach something better due to the compromises upon which they have built their lives. This is because they have based their lives upon their aptitudes, not their true desires. For many, some talent they happened to possess at age fourteen determined their life direction.

Of course, the deeper basic premise of this type of guidance counseling is that people cannot learn and develop unless they already have gifts built into the circuitry. According to this mentality, your true desires don't count. You should base your life upon your aptitude, no matter what you want. But true desires don't go away simply because they are ignored. They go underground, waiting for a full-fledged midlife crisis to set them free.

The Conflict Between Freedom and Obligation

Here is a basic, yet profound, question: *if you have talents and abilities, are you obligated to develop them?* Or, are you free to live your life the way you see fit, pursuing your own aspirations, independent of your talents and abilities?

Do people with fewer gifts have less responsibility and obligation in their lives? Are they freer than someone with great talent and abilities? If that were so, many people would wish for fewer gifts, because their talents and abilities would end up controlling their destiny.

Must all of your potential seek perfect realization?

Do you have to use your gifts?

If your Aunt Sally gave you a horrendous pair of pajamas for Christmas, do you have to wear them?

If you have a gift for playing the harmonica, do you have to play the harmonica?

WHAT YOU SHOULD GET OUT OF THIS CHAPTER

- Perfection is a silly goal, and it is impossible to reach.
- Perfection itself implies a built-in criticism of life as it actually is.
- Better than perfection is the appreciation of the irony, flaws, and imperfections of life as it exists.
- Too many people have their identities tied up with the ideal of perfection.
- If you have talent, are you obligated to use it, or is it your free choice?
- Too often, people think they have a duty to their talents.
- If talents and abilities are true gifts, you can use them as you want to. You are not obligated simply by their presence.

Chapter 8

ROLES AND STEREOTYPES

The Macho Thing

The authors of this book have always hated the prevailing notion of how you are supposed to be as a man. In a parallel universe, there exists the counterpoint of how you are supposed to be if you are a woman; but frankly, the "man" one hits closer to home for the authors personally.

In many cultures, male children are asked to conform to various images of "manhood." Too often, these images are nothing more than a stereotyped distortion, reduced to a simplistic ideal. According to the American Psychological Association, behavior compatible with cultural expectation is called "gender-normative." Behavior incompatible with these expectations is termed "non-conformity." Let's break this down.

The first idea has to do with *cultural expectations.*

Where do these expectations come from? Certainly, they develop over time within the culture. We can see that various primordial tribes, ones that have little contact with the modern world, often hold vastly different sets of expectations.

These expectations are an invention, not an evolutionary fact of nature. In many cultures, real men wear pants; yet men in Scotland also wear kilts, and in Bhutan, they wear the *gho*. The variety is endless.

The next idea is *conformity*. Within the context of expectation, one has a choice to go along with it or not. Perhaps the word "choice" is misleading. Often, there is no sense of a conscious choice when it comes to cultural gender compliance. Some people find themselves falling into conformity, while others find themselves out of step with prevailing cultural norms. Many who do not naturally conform have one of two choices: to pretend to conform, or to be a non-conformist.

If you have a gender ideal, you have an identity issue. As a man, you would have an undue focus upon who you are as a man. (The same is true for females who have gender ideals. Your focus would be on who you are as a woman.)

Some men are more physically adventurous than others. Same for women. That doesn't have any meaning in particular, except that some people demonstrate a predisposition toward certain things, like racecar driving, football, hang gliding, or scuba diving—and others don't. *There is no right way to be a man or a woman.* People who would impose a fixed image upon gender identity are trying to define what is and is not acceptable. What is the source of their authority? Who gives them the right to dictate how anyone should be?

Nowadays, there are some people who complain about the "feminization" of boys. An extreme expression of this comes from the book, *Raising Boys Feminists Will Hate*, by Doug Giles. He writes:

> "Parent, if you have a young son and you want him to grow up to be a man, then you need to keep him away from pop culture, feminized public schools, and...

> the effeminate branches of evangelicalism....If [they] lay their sissy hands on him, you can kiss masculinity goodbye, because they will morph him into a dandy. Yeah, Mom and Dad, if—if—you dare to raise your boy as a classic boy in this castrated epoch, then you've got a task that's more difficult than getting a drunk to hit the urinal at Chili's."

This over-the-top canon of what it means to be a "real" man produces a cartoon caricature of some kind of Rambo individual, a fictional character invented by Sylvester Stallone. Rambo is not its creator. Notice that Rambo didn't go into theater and film, as did Stallone, nor did he develop his screen-writing skills or direct feature films or play in off-Broadway shows—something we might imagine Giles would not want his son to do if he had sons (he has two daughters.) The message is clear: here is the macho ideal you have to live up to if you are a boy.

The superficial is the enemy of the authentic. It is easier to take on the manner of things rather than their substance; so the next time someone tries to tell you that you are not this or that ENOUGH, or that if you raise boys, they should be treated one way, and if you raise girls, they should be treated another, realize that the point itself is not about real life, but about an idealized image of identity.

These days, in public life, an idealized image of the virtue of courage connects with masculine gender identity. It is not unusual to hear politicians say, "Man up." If they don't like the opposition, they accuse their competitor, man or woman, of not being "man enough." In other words, the only reason one might disagree with a policy is because of a person's sexual identity. Thanks for elevating the conversation to a higher level, you class acts, you.

Roles and Stereotypes

It is easy to assume that we have defined roles as men or women. These roles come from a few influential sources: family, mass media, teachers, and society. Most people conform to socially-acceptable stereotypes; therefore, there exists little dissonance between what is expected and what most people experience, from a gender point of view. The World Health Organization defines gender roles as "socially-constructed roles, behaviors, activities, and attributes that a given society considers appropriate for men and women." In other words, it's a roll-your-own world. In one social order, the image of what it means to be a man is vastly different from that of another society. The same applies to women. These social norms become an image of identity. A member of society has one of two choices: conform or rebel. Who you are as a man or woman is answered by how well you fit the stereotype. The stereotype is a social invention of pure fiction, made to seem as if it is true science. While it may *seem* as if it is a biological fact of life that men are this way and women are that way, the stereotype is hardly based upon biology; rather, it is based upon social models evolved over time within the social order.

Yet there are biological differences between men and women. Numerous researchers have noted statistical variations—for example, in verbal and mathematical abilities. Hartung & Widiger (1998) found that there were gender differences in various mental illnesses and behavioral problems. "Of the 80 disorders diagnosed in adulthood for which sex ratios are provided, 35 are said to be more common in men than in women, 31 are said to be more common in women than men, and 14 are said to be equally common in both sexes."

A 2008 research project found that, for grades 2 to 11, there were no significant gender differences in math skills among the general population. There are, of course, women engineers and mathematicians, and it often said that some of the best chefs are men. So what is the real story? While there may be gender differences in overall predisposition (spatial/temporal, rational/intuitive, etc.), it is when we get to the individual that statistics fail to reflect real life. What does it matter if most men are better at spatial relationships? What does it matter that most women are better at perceptual speed at identifying objects, or that most men are better at target-directed motor skills, such as throwing darts, and most women are better at recall? Statistics tell the story of averages: using a vantage point over a wide range of possibilities. Your personal profile will be unique to you, independent of anyone else. There is no "right" way to be a man or a woman. There is just your way—and that is not a matter of identity or statistics. Qualities like these say nothing about who you are.

The Feminine Mystique—Revisited

Over half a century ago, Betty Friedan made history with the publication of her classic book, *The Feminine Mystique*. What she discovered was that American women in the 1950s and 1960s were presented with an ideal—the prototypical housewife, homemaker, mother and wife—and if women lived up to this ideal, they would be happy. As Friedan's research discovered, these women were not happy at all. Instead, they were living lives of quiet desperation.

There was a very different image for women in 1930s film, radio, and advertising: the typical Rosalind Russell role, the fast-talking, strong career woman, often a newspaper reporter, judge, psychiatrist. She was ten times smarter than the men around her—especially the love interest who was always trying to slow her down and make her into a housewife, something she refused to do. Even though she might marry the guy, she never considered giving up her career. Her greatest commitment was to be true to herself, her values, and her aspirations.

Other such role models playing these parts included Myrna Loy, Greta Garbo, Carole Lombard, Marlene Dietrich, Barbara Stanwyck, Betty Davis, Katherine Hepburn, Joan Crawford, Mary Astor...the list goes on. These actresses were not cast as stay-at-home ladies concerned with how clean their kitchen floor was, or whether dinner was on the table at the same time each night.

Women of the 1950s often held a built-in existential crisis: a conflict between who they were supposed to be and what was supposed to make them happy, against the reality of a pattern of lack of fulfillment and chronic depression.

The feminist movement of the 1960s embodied a typical reaction to the previous period—to redefine the role of women as strong, independent, a force of nature, and people not to be messed with. As usual, the reaction presented as much of a two-dimensional cartoon caricature as that which it was working against. That's because reactions to convention are predictably militant, at first. The word *girl* was outlawed. Now it was a "ten-year-old young *woman*." After a few years and a lot of bras put to flame, something began to come through that was serious and truthful—and that was the emergence of the deepest desires of both women and men to create their own lives as best they could. The feminist movement did serve to change discriminatory laws and practices. More people became aware of gender prejudice, and many women found it easier to enter professions such as medicine, engineering, politics, construction, and business. Biases against women remain, especially in the ranks of corporate leadership. In a survey taken in 2013, only 16.9% of women sit on corporate boards; and, as of this writing, women only hold 5.2% of CEO positions in *Fortune*'s top 1000 CEOs.

Society is not to be trusted when it comes to assigning roles for people. Typically, the roles it assigns are tied to identity: "Here is who you are and who you are supposed to be. Don't try to be anything else." If one waited for the social order to grant freedom of choice, one would have to wait forever.

Yet not all social changes require a revolution or a movement. This branch of social change requires each person to do some soul-searching about how he or she chooses to live his or her life. It must be remembered that BOTH men and women have been put into boxes of identity and role, through social images and built-in assumptions about what our jobs are in life.

It is important to recognize that women have been oppressed throughout history. Most societies see women as second-class citizens, incapable of equality with men. Even in today's world, many societies oppress women. This oppression comes from social stereotypes that see women as inferior to men, and divides gender into identity roles. That's sad on two counts. One is the fact that a vast pool of talent available to a society is now inaccessible. The other is that identity, rather than a person's actual individual merit, pigeonholes her into confined boxes, limiting her choices in life. If we look at history, the facts are all there. Women have led countries, and have been groundbreaking scientists, astronauts, business leaders, doctors, surgeons, and inventors; women have excelled at just about anything men can do. There is no lack of potential, just an ongoing social limitation based upon gender identity.

Of course, there are some pretty fundamental differences between men and women, but these differences do not justify limitations to self-determination, freedom, or equality of opportunity. It makes sense for women to demand equality; but this demand is not about identity. Rather, it is about justice, freedom, and equal rights for the individual. And women are not the only ones who want to support such things. You could be anyone, of any background, gender, age, upbringing, social class, personal history, experience, training, or credentials—anyone, anywhere. There is nothing especially masculine or feminine motivating the desire for equality, freedom and justice. What if there were no considerations of identity whatsoever? How might the quality of everyone's lives change? How much better a society might we be able to create?

WHAT YOU SHOULD GET OUT OF THIS CHAPTER

- Too often, stereotypes dictate how to be the gender that you are.
- These stereotypes are cultural inventions rather than universal truths.
- Both men and women are forced into stereotypes as part of their identity.
- There is no right way to be a man or a woman.
- Society is not to be trusted when it comes to assigning roles to people.
- Differences between men and women do not justify limitations to self-determination, freedom, and equal opportunity.

Chapter 9

TRYING TO JUSTIFY YOUR EXISTENCE

Many people are in the bad habit of judging themselves against how much they have done during the day, or the week, or up to a certain point in their lives. They have tied their accomplishments to their identity, and these accomplishments have a specific function in their lives: to justify their existence. If they have done enough good things, they deserve to live; but ironically, there are never enough good things to finally succeed in justifying their existence. For some, a critical evaluation takes place at the end of the day: "I did enough today," or "I didn't do enough today."

The need to justify one's existence is based upon a set of assumptions. The first is that you have no value, in and of yourself. Your worth is tied to the good deeds you can offer the world. People who make this assumption can never take pride in a job well done. Instead, as if there were a good-deed bank account with their name on it, they simply add items to the ledger. The second assumption is that no matter how many good deeds you've done in the past, it's never enough.

You need to continue to find ways of justifying your existence forever. Sometimes, people call this *giving back*; at other times, they call it *paying on account*. Built into these assumptions is the belief that one's life needs to be validated according to how much he or she has contributed to others, or to the world.

George Bernard Shaw said:

> "You must all know half a dozen people at least who are no use in this world; who are more trouble than they are worth. Just put them there, and say, now, Sir or Madam, now will you be kind enough to justify your existence? If you can't justify your existence; if you're not pulling your weight in the social boat; if you're not producing as much as you consume or perhaps a little more, then clearly we cannot use the big organization of our society or the purpose of keeping you alive, because your life does not benefit us, and it can't be of very much use to yourself."

As exaggerated as this statement may sound, many people agree with its underlying assumptions: that your worth comes from pulling your own weight, and if you're not, there is no reason to exist.

If this is the case, you have created or adopted a myth, one all of us have been fed from the time we were toddlers: that we have a job in life, and that is to achieve something of value. We are praised if we succeed, and criticized if we fail. We learn to take it personally. Success or failure takes on specific meaning. We are good or bad, depending upon our level of accomplishment. This myth can become so ingrained in us that it goes without saying. It becomes an invisible assumption, one we may hold, but one that we do not know we are holding.

Perfectly wonderful people can feel deep-seated guilt when they have done nothing wrong. They simply think they haven't done enough. Of course, soon there is a backlog of times they haven't done enough, and the feeling that there is something wrong with them begins to permeate their lives.

Eric Hoffer said, "The individual who has to justify his existence by his own efforts is in eternal bondage to himself."

Here are some questions for you to explore. Try to answer them as honestly as you can, perhaps looking deeper and in a more penetrating way than usual.

- Do you try to define yourself by your accomplishments?
- Do you think you are a better person if you succeed, and not as good a person if you fail?
- Do you think you have a mission in life, but that you don't know what it is—and, therefore, you are not living up to it?
- Do you feel you have a mission in life, but that you aren't doing enough to fulfill it?
- Do you feel you need to do more than you do?

If you answered "yes" to any of these questions, you are putting a burden on yourself that arises from the misconceptions you have picked up somewhere along the way in your life.

It doesn't matter where you may have taken on these concepts. What matters is that you have adopted them, and think they are true—which they are not. Concepts are not reality. The life-building process happens in reality. Remember, the essence of structural tension is rather simple: What do you want to create? Where are you now in relation to that outcome? What actions do you need to take to accomplish that outcome? Notice that the answers to these questions have no place for your self-concept…or any other type of concept. Your successes do not justify your existence, nor do your good works—or anything else you can do, make, accomplish, invent, develop, contribute, support, or achieve.

You Cannot Justify Your Existence

The concepts you hold are not factual reality. They are simply your impressions of reality, which include the assumptions you make, the ideals you hold, the models you adopt, and the various myths that have infiltrated your mind over the years. In reality, you exist. Period. An explanation of WHY you exist can only be answered by a concept. Of course, we could cite the biological mechanisms—egg, sperm, etc.—but that is the HOW, not the WHY. In fact, while there are a lot of theories about why we exist, all of them speculate based upon concepts. None of them can be proven objectively.

If we don't know *why* we exist, but just that we *do*, how can we say that one thing or another can justify the fact of our existence? Does the person who finds the cure for cancer have more of a claim to exist than the cancer patient? And just who is the judge about this? The fact is, you cannot justify your existence any more than a bird, or a dog, or a cow, or a crow, or a grain of rice, or a tree, or the stars. Human beings can be very inventive in the ways they create myths about true mysteries. In light of not knowing the reason for existence, we fabricate lofty-sounding concepts.

Now, if the previous thought were true, what implications does that have for your life? In one profound transformation, you could open a new world of freedom of choice. Your identity would not be linked to your accomplishments. You could think in terms of what you truly want, not how well what you do justifies your existence or how it makes you look. You might discover that you still want some very noble things. Even though this will not justify your existence, you may still want to contribute to other people's lives, support their successes, invent cures for diseases, help the needy, advance the arts, and do what you can to make the world a better place. These acts no longer have the ulterior motive of justifying your existence. They become true acts of altruism, done for their own sake, because that was your true desire.

Reminder: You are not your successes or failures, good deeds, accomplishments, or even your altruism. You are also not your laziness, lethargy, or idleness. You cannot be that which you possess.

WHAT YOU SHOULD GET OUT OF THIS CHAPTER

- Many people think they need to justify their existence with good works and valuable contributions to society.
- The fact is, you exist.
- Nothing you can do, no matter how good, can justify your existence, because it does not need to be justified.
- We don't know why we exist, even though there are countless theories, and countless people who are happy to tell you why we do.
- You are not anything you do or accomplish. Therefore, even if you contribute wonderful works to the world, you are not those accomplishments.
- You are free from that job!

Chapter 10

CREATOR – CREATION

ONE WAY TO UNDERSTAND your motivation involves making a distinction between you as *creator* (the person making things happen) and your *creation* (the outcomes you create).

Your creation may be a work of art, a business, a family, a building, or a book; but more importantly, your creation can be your own life. The creative process is the most successful process for accomplishment in history. As we've said, it has created the arts, science, technology, and so much more. Doesn't it make sense to use the most successful process in history to create your own life?

Creators come in many forms, from amateurs who write an occasional poem, or put together a flower arrangement, or decorate a patio outside the house, or write a blog—to consummate professionals such as screenwriters, architects, inventors, engineers, artists, composers, fashion designers, and so on.

People who make their living as creators are often clear about the separation between themselves and the things they are creating. This separation is critical, because it enables you to review your own work and process objectively. From there, you are able to learn, adjust future actions, and build experience and momentum.

Non-professionals often have a different orientation. They can confuse what they have created with themselves. Those of you with identity issues may think that everything you create says something about you. This makes it hard to be objective, learn, adjust, improve, and reach more and more of the results you want to create. If you think you are what you create, it can be hard not to take everything you do personally.

In this chapter, we are offering you one giant step toward a better orientation—one in which you are able to position yourself to learn, grow, develop, and create the life you want to live.

We begin with two elements: *the creator*, and *that which is created*. What is the relationship between these two elements?

Here are two ways it can go:

The Focus is on the Creator

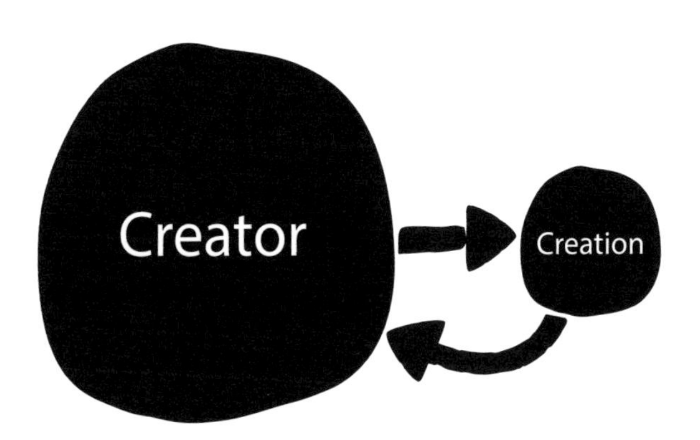

In this diagram, the reason for creation is centered around *you*. The motivation is the famous "return on investment"— in other words, what the creation gives *you*, how it makes *you* feel, what it says about *you*.

In our society, return on investment is considered *the* "correct" motivation. We have been taught to think in terms of *what's in it for number one?* The questions TV interviewers ask people who have done wonderful things are usually about the benefits of their experience. Acceptable answers include comments like: "It was fun," or "It gave me great satisfaction." The general agreement about human nature is that we do what we do for the rewards our actions bring. In the book *Punished by Rewards*, author Alfie Kohn writes:

> "Within the discipline of psychology, the passive-organism view has faded along with the influence of behavior theory itself. But in everyday life, in the workplace and the classroom and the home, this view continues to make its presence felt through the practices of pop behaviorism. To put this the other way around, our everyday practices rest on an implicit theory of human nature that fails to do us justice. When we repeatedly promise rewards to children for acting responsibly, or to students for making an effort to learn something new, or to employees for doing quality work, we are assuming that they could not or would not choose to act this way on their own."

The notion that we do what we do for a return on investment negatively influences our ability to be involved with our own lives. When, in time, do you know if your involvement has paid off? When do you know that it has given us the satisfaction, fun, validation, credibility, or even the financial reward we were hoping for? Only *after* the fact, at the end of the process, once it is over and complete. Until then, we don't know if it will pay off, so we will always be checking it out. *Will it do it for me? Is this worth it?* Until we know that, we can't be fully involved.

You can be fully involved when you are focused upon the success of the *outcome* you are trying to achieve rather than the rewards it may provide. Here is a different orientation, one in which the focus is on the creation rather than the creator.

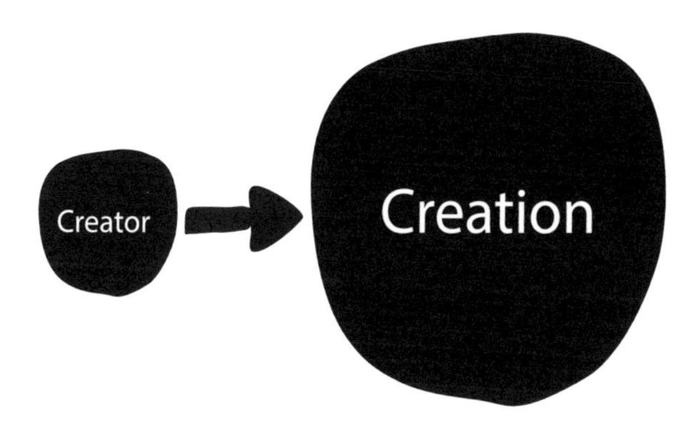

Our society has been so indoctrinated with the return on investment mentality that it is hard for many to understand that often, our best motivation comes from a focus on the results we create, rather than on ourselves. The creator/CREATION orientation is common, but often goes unrecognized. Parents truly understand this motivation. They take their children to Music Together® classes or Little League or Disney World, not because they expect that in some distant future the kids will return the favor by becoming rich musicians or athletes who can take care of them in their old age, or even for the hope of a "thank you," but because they love their kids and want the best for them. Poet Robert Frost put it this way: "All the great things are done for their own sake." Edgar Allan Poe, in his essay "The Poetic Principle," wrote, "...this poem, which is a poem and nothing more, this poem written solely for the poem's sake." Art for art's sake comes from the French slogan *l'art pour l'art*, which expresses the idea that the intrinsic value of art, and the only "true" art, is divorced from any utilitarian function, such as message art or political art.

Can this same principle be the basis for living one's life—life for life's sake? If we understand that you are not your life, but something you create, the idea begins to take on new possibilities. The painter is separate from the painting, and, because of that, he or she can make adjustments, change approach, rethink the painting, and learn. If the painter had his or her identity confused with the painting, it would be harder to evaluate how closely the reality of the painting comes to the vision of the final result. As the painter knows, he or she is not the painting; and *you* can know that you are not the life you are creating.

There might be a great return on investment on some of the things you are creating. Rock stars make a lot of money, gain tons of admiration, and are treated as if they are special wherever they go. They have what could be described as wonderful return on investment, but the point of being a rock star is not for those benefits. It is for the music. In Jackson Browne's song "The Load-Out," he describes the things they have on the band bus—music, movies, truckers on CB radio:

But the only time that seems too short
Is the time that we get to play…

We just pass the time in our hotel rooms
And wander 'round backstage
Till those lights come up and we hear that crowd
And we remember why we came

—Jackson Browne

Often, people say that the reason they did the great thing was for the satisfaction it gave them; however, some days we're satisfied, and some days we're not. Satisfaction comes and goes. If you do something for the satisfaction, know that it won't last long. You can't be satisfied on days you are unsatisfied—but when your orientation is on *creation* rather than *yourself*, you *can be* fully involved. You can be involved on the good days, the bad days, and everything in between. You can be involved on days you are satisfied AND days you are not satisfied, happy, or inspired. For most people, involvement is more important than satisfaction.

For some, success is simply achieving a desired outcome. While success is more desirable than failure, success or failure say nothing whatsoever about the person. Success is almost always the better side of the coin, and failure can be a learning experience that often leads to future success; but when a person has an identity issue in which success and failure are taken personally, learning is limited, and reality becomes distorted to the point where it is hard to make effective decisions on behalf of one's desired goals. Here are some common strategies that people use to deal with failure when it is tied to their identity. See if you do any of these:

- Claim the failure was actually a success.
- Talk about what a useful lesson failure is ("Good things always come from these challenges.")
- Blame others ("It wasn't my fault.")
- Blame destiny or karma.
- Blame a rigged game.
- Try to convince yourself it didn't matter anyway (sour grapes)

- Engage in "if only" thinking ("If only I had more time…")
- Beat yourself up to warn yourself to be better next time.

As we've said, failure is part of life. It comes with the territory of learning and growing, but when you take it personally, it's hard to enjoy the benefits of the lessons that may be critical to your future success.

The Focus

One theme of this book involves changing your focus from yourself to the outcomes you are working to achieve. This is easy to say and understand as a message, but harder to do. It takes a degree of self-discipline and self-awareness to accomplish this change of focus. A new skill or habit is developed in stages, and it is easy to fall into reactive patterns. As Stella Adler said to her acting students, "Nothing in theater is personal." And actor and acting coach Todd Bruno has said, "You have to leave your ego at home. Realize it's not about you, it's about the project."

WHAT YOU SHOULD GET OUT OF THIS CHAPTER

- There are two basic orientations you can have: return on investment or working on behalf of the existence of the creation.
- When the goal is return on investment, you can't know if it did the job until it's over. Therefore, it is hard for you to fully be involved.
- People with identity issues want their return on investment to be that their success says something about them personally.
- When the focus is on the creation itself, it is possible to be totally involved.
- People want involvement more than they want satisfaction, which never lasts.
- To shift from one orientation to the other, refocus yourself on the outcomes you are creating, not what it might be doing for you.

Chapter 11

THE MARSHMALLOW TEST

In the 1960s, Walter Mischel, a professor at Stanford University, offered a number of children a marshmallow. Each test subject was given the same bargain. If he or she waited 15 minutes before eating the marshmallow, he or she would get another marshmallow. Some children waited, others did not.

The significance of this test became clear years later. The children who waited had better and more productive lives than the ones who ate the marshmallow right away. Their SAT scores were much higher, their body mass index was lower, and their overall life achievement was much better. These are profound differences; yet a full understanding of the causes involved in this difference, and how this difference might be predictive of future success or failure, is usually missed.

There are structural dynamics at play here. Each child was subject to the structure he or she was in. For some children, the immediate craving for the marshmallow demanded instant gratification. They had no sense of future. To them, everything seemed to exist right now. Their craving was a tension that demanded to be resolved immediately, and the major dynamic in the situation was to satisfy their impulsive hunger. Their time frame was in the here and now, and the future seemed vague and distant. To them, the thought of twice as many marshmallows was abstract and vague in contrast with the actual marshmallow that was right there in front of them.

Those who did wait were living in a different time frame. They understood things from a broader perspective. The experience of time included a sense of past into the present, and on into the future. They were able to connect current actions with future consequences. They were able to focus upon their longer-range desires rather than their immediate instincts, impulses, and appetites. This is how the structural dynamics worked for them: the thought of eating two marshmallows (a different tension than the craving) led them to *delay the resolution*. In other words, those children were able to understand that their more important goal was to have twice as many marshmallows; and to support that goal, they did not succumb to the temptation of the marshmallow in front of them.

As it turned out, over the next 30 or 40 years, the patterns didn't seem to change. If the child had eaten the marshmallow right away, he or she was impulsive, instinctive, and subject to various appetites. If the child had delayed eating the marshmallow, that person was able to create many positive benefits and accomplishments within his or her life, because the focal point was longer-range aspirations and values.

Are our life patterns fused into us when we are young, as the marshmallow test implies? Are we stuck? Can we change? And if so, what would motivate that change? From our work in structural dynamics, we find that you CAN change your basic orientation, no matter how long you've been a different structure. You can learn how to delay resolution of tensions strategically, so that you have a better chance at accomplishing your more important goals and aspirations; but there is a common misconception about how to engineer such a change. The medical profession has come to the general conclusion that you cannot change people's lifestyle habits. People have been asked to eat better, exercise, and take on other lifestyle habits for decades by well-meaning doctors. Very few of their patients take this advice permanently. If they can't change their habits to healthier ones, then the next-best choice is drug therapies. If they can't eat a diet that is healthy for diabetics, then give them pharmaceuticals. If they can't stop overeating, then get lap band surgery. If their weight makes it difficult to walk, give them electric-powered mobility scooters.

Until now, doctors have had only two methods available to them in order to try to change people's habits: conflict manipulation and willpower manipulation.

Conflict Manipulation

In the hands of a doctor, the usual warning goes like this: "Give up smoking or die." To the diabetic, it's "Eat the right foods, or we may have to amputate your leg." This tactic puts pressure on the patient by painting visions of an early death or terrible suffering. The hope is that the patient will react to the conflict he or she feels, and change the bad habits. Often, the patient does, in fact, react by adopting the new health regime; but the structural dynamics are against sustainable change. Here's why: the reason you would change your habit and adopt the new, healthier behavior is because you feel emotional conflict generated by visions of negative consequences. Once you begin to take action, the experience of emotional conflict is reduced: less emotional conflict, less motivation to continue the good behavior. Soon, you have reverted back to your old habits.

Here's a truism: *All change motivated by conflict will be temporary.*

As Robert Frost said, "I never tried to worry anybody into intelligence." Yet most change efforts do exactly that: here are all the terrible things that will happen unless you act. And so you take action, but it is hard to sustain the pressure. The next time you find yourself caught up in guilt trips, warnings, admonishments, and pressuring yourself, know that this approach will not help you change for good.

Willpower Manipulation

The other side of the coin is willpower manipulation. Instead of trying to create visions of disaster, we create visions of fantastic rewards, and convince ourselves to have enough determination and force. We are told, through pep talks, affirmations, positive thinking, or encouragement to overcome barriers, that we can reach the goal. In fact, it is possible to reach your goal; but once reached, the goal is unsustainable. Remember the two rubber bands; once you reach the other side of the room, the rubber band behind you is pulling you away in the opposite direction from your goal. If your identity is tied up with your accomplishments, reaching the goal is the hardest point to maintain, because the other rubber band is moving you away from where you want to be.

We have pointed out the boomerang effect and the limitations of positive thinking. Additionally, you need to be fluent in reality if you are to accomplish your goals. Any distortion of reality makes it harder to achieve sustainable success.

The children who did not wait the 15 minutes had less-productive lives than those who did. That's because they did not change their underlying structure. This was through no fault of their own; they didn't know there was a structure in place that was not conducive to success. If they could have changed their underlying structure, they could have changed their life direction. That statement is true because of this principle: a change in structure leads to a change in behavior. In this book, we are addressing this type of change.

The Marshmallow Test concludes that once people are formed at an early age, they cannot change. They are stuck; game over. Yet if we refocus from short-term impulses and appetites to longer-term aspirations and values, there can be a change of structure. We can strategically delay instant gratification on behalf of more important goals. To do this, we need to develop a new ability: to create *hierarchy*. Hierarchy means that we are sorting out how important things are. What is more important to you? What is less important to you?

Let's think this through. We have one of two choices: acting for immediate gratification, or acting for longer-term desired outcomes. Often, in reality, we want two things that are mutually exclusive. We want to be thin and healthy, and we want to eat everything in sight. We want to gain the benefits of exercise, and we want to be couch potatoes in front of the TV. It's good to tell ourselves the truth: we want them *both*, but they are mutually exclusive. We can't have both, so the question becomes, which one do we want *more*?

Usually, we want the longer-term goal more than the shorter-term one; but it is so easy to slip into appetites, impulses, and instincts, and act in ways that are contradictory to our larger aspirations. Knowing that we have this tendency, we can create a strategy well before we face the temptation of instant gratification. Once we know it's coming—and that we can be suckers for that donut, cake, or Big Mac®, we can decide which is more important to us: the momentary pleasure of satisfying our appetites or instincts, or supporting our more important, longer-range goals.

Here is where the power of structural tension comes in. Once we establish structural tension by understanding our longer-term goals in relation to our current reality, it becomes obvious which actions can best support the cause, and which actions get in the way. We can make strategic choices that support our more important goals.

Primary and Secondary Choices

Once you know your primary choice—the major outcome you want to create—the choice itself generates a series of other strategic choices. If you want optimal health, there will be other choices that may include eating habits, exercise, adequate sleep, and so on. Primary means *first*. Other choices come second, and, accordingly, are called *secondary choices*. Often, secondary choices are not actions you would take for their own sake, but because they support the higher-order primary choice.

The key to discipline is making primary and secondary choices, and this type of discipline leads to long-term success. It is not what you think (your beliefs and concepts), as the self-help people claim. Rather, it is what you do, the actions you take, and the deeper motivation for these actions. In the case of your life-building process, the motivation exists because you want to see the outcomes you desire. Then, you are able to delay the immediate demands that are always bombarding you in favor of the things that truly support what matters most to you.

No matter what your past patterns have been, you can create an underlying structure that supports your highest aspirations and values. Here are the key ingredients: structural tension (knowing the outcome you want to create and its current, relevant reality); making strategic primary and secondary choices; and keeping the focus on your desired end results, not on yourself.

WHAT YOU SHOULD GET OUT OF THIS CHAPTER

- When appetites, impulses, and instincts are the major focus, short-term goals, rather than longer-term aspirations and values, demand quick gratification.
- When longer-term aspirations and values are the focus, it is easier to make strategic secondary choices on behalf of your more important interests.
- How you have been does not determine how you will be.
- This is not a matter of your personal identity, but rather the structure you are in.
- Structural tension is the key ingredient to long-term success.

Chapter 12

BUT I BEAT MYSELF UP...

UNTIL NOW, we have focused on people trying to uphold their idealized self-image with tactics of positive reinforcement and attempts to love themselves. There is another side of the same coin, in which the behavior is exactly the opposite. In this case, the person is quite aware of feeling like a fraud, not good enough, not capable or competent, less than most other people, or obsessed with insecurities—what used to be called, in another era, an inferiority complex.

The very same structure that produces the Ideal/Belief/Reality conflict is at the heart of this issue. The difference is that the person is well aware of his or her unwanted belief. Given that it is unacceptable, instead of trying to ignore it, the person amplifies it.

For those who have this going on, the point of the strategy is to create enough emotional conflict to warn themselves against what they think they would do if left to their own devices. If you thought you were a kleptomaniac, for example, you would have to remind yourself of that fact; when visiting your rich uncle Henry for a dinner party, you would have to warn yourself not to steal the silverware.

Another Example of Conflict Manipulation

Self-management based upon warnings and cautions illustrates another example of conflict manipulation—the form we explored in the previous chapter. If you thought you were out of control, for example, you might warn yourself to behave well: "You'd better be in control when you go to the meeting today."

"You'd better keep your big mouth shut at the PTA meeting."

"You'd better watch yourself at airport security so you don't make stupid jokes about hijacking an airliner."

Many people with this strategy try to maintain a constant high level of pressure on themselves. They beat themselves up with some of the most vicious self-admonishment one can imagine.

Congressman Tim Ryan was one of the youngest people to have been elected to the Ohio Senate, and was elected to the U.S. Congress at age 29. Here is what he writes in his book, *Mindful Nation:*

> "The thoughts continued to be judgmental and critical. In fact, they were mean. It became apparent to me that such thoughts tend to reoccur. They can be like background noise. I had just never noticed them. As they revealed themselves to me, I realized I could be terribly hard on myself. I could judge myself with a level of cruelty I wouldn't inflict on my worst enemy. I could get stuck in a thought loop of questioning past decisions

or regretting remarks I made or lines in speeches I'd given. It was repeated pressure, always self-imposed. I thought I was kind, compassionate, and considerate. It turns out that was true only if I was dealing with someone other than myself. But toward myself I could be cruel, unforgiving, dissatisfied, manipulative, mean-spirited, and needlessly judgmental. I started to think about my new nephew and how I would never treat him this way. Toward everyone else I was the town nice guy; to myself I was the town asshole.

It turns out that over the years, I unknowingly created a big story in my head. I shared it with no one, not even my own conscious mind. I needed to have a highly successful political career, marry the perfect woman, be worth millions of dollars, and write a few books and movies. And if I didn't do all of this, my family and friends would see me as an underachiever. How tiring! I couldn't believe I spent so much time and energy trying to uphold a story I created in my own head."

Notice the ideal he created for himself: have a successful political career, the perfect wife, be a millionaire, an author, and a screenwriter. In many ways, these function as *symbols of success* rather than true aspirations. What a contrast to the "town asshole" he thought himself to be. He used his unwanted beliefs about himself as a bat to hammer himself into good behavior. The organizing thought here was *Here's how I am, and I'd better not be that way.*

Of course, Ryan is not alone in this strategy. The focus is on your identity, and the fear is that other people will find out the awful truth about you. It becomes important to wear a mask, yet the mask makes it next to impossible to have a real relationship with anyone, because one of you is missing: *you.* The closer the relationship seems to become, the more pressure there is to hide from that person. This cycle reinforces the concept of what a terrible person you must be, that you cannot let anyone see you as you really are. You become isolated even when you are with groups of people in social and professional situations. The feeling *there's something wrong with me* permeates everything you do, think, feel, and experience. You become a stranger in a strange land.

Understand that this structure is caused not by the unwanted belief alone; simultaneously, you have aspirations, values, desires, and a strong, dynamic urge to accomplish things that matter to you. If you didn't want to get somewhere in life, there would be no need to beat yourself up.

Of course, when people have adopted the strategy of conflict manipulation, they are told things like *be nice to yourself,* or *you need to learn to love yourself,* or *you should say affirmations about how wonderful you are.* If we consider the underlying structure the person is in, we can understand why these bromides backfire. Even as the person tries to give him- or herself a pep talk, the belief becomes more in-focus. People who have this structure would love to love themselves, be accepting of their flaws, and think that they are wonderful and brilliant—they just don't.

Objective vs. Subjective Criticism

There exists a vast difference between subjective and objective criticism. *Subjective criticism* functions to evoke emotional conflict—which, in turn, is designed to manipulate one into better behavior.

Objective criticism has the goal of evaluating how well you did in any given situation, so you can understand what worked and what didn't. This leads to learning how to improve your ability to be more successful, next time out.

The more your identity is a factor, the less you are able to be objective. What would happen if your identity were not a factor? You could observe, learn, improve, see the kind of help you might need from others, see which skills you need to develop, and understand the knowledge and experience you need to acquire. Objective evaluation functions as an essential ingredient in your life-building process. With it, everything becomes an experiment. "Let's see what happens when I do this. Let's see what happens when I do that." Success and failure lead equally to knowledge about how to become more effective. Neither outcome is taken personally.

Here's an example of typical *internal* dialogue, when identity is tied to action.

Let's see, I need to move the couch to the left.
You should have known that before it was put there, so you wouldn't have to move it.
Yeah, but...
Okay, so move it.
Right, so I'll begin to move it. Oh, it's heavy.
You weakling. Bad diet, no exercise, what do you expect, you couch potato, trying to move a couch?
Maybe I need help.
What? You can't move a little couch all by yourself? What's wrong with you?
Just a little more...and...
You put it in the wrong place again. Idiot! How stupid can you be?

Pretty stupid, now that I mention it.
Remember last week, when you strained your back because you didn't have the sense to get someone to help you move that heavy trunk?
So, I'd better face facts. I am a puny loser who can't even move a trunk, let alone a couch. And when I do move it, it is in the wrong place.
Yeah, you are one hell of an idiot.

When it is not about you, the internal dialogue is different:

Let's see, I need to move the couch to the left.
That means when I placed it there, I didn't have the right idea.
So, is the right idea moving it to the left? Let's find out.
Hmm. It is heavier than I thought. I wonder if I should get someone to help me?
Well, let me give it a try, and if it turns out to be too much, I'll ask Joe to help.
Okay, okay. Little by little. Okay. Now it's where I thought it should be. Let's take a step back and see if that did the job. Looks better, but not quite right yet. Okay, what is missing? What adjustments need to happen? I could move even more to the left. Before I do that, let me imagine that, and see what it looks like in my mind. Ah, it looks like it might work. Okay, just a little movement at a time, and now, it's in place. Let's move back and see what that did.

Notice that the internal thoughts expressed in the above dialogue are about the placement of the couch, and not about the person him- or herself.

Manipulation

The reasoning behind manipulating yourself comes from the assumption that, left to your own devices, you would NOT do the right thing. People with identity issues think they are not inherently motivated to act correctly, so they must force themselves to do the right thing with warnings, on the one hand, or pep talks, on the other. There is no shortage of advice about how you should behave based upon the concept that, on your own, you would not do the "right thing."

Here are some famous quotes that contain some form of manipulation:

> "If you're not part of the solution, you're part of the problem."
> —*Eldridge Cleaver*

Here, you can play one of only two available roles, and one of them is unacceptable. The idea is simple enough: be "part of the solution," usually by joining the cause of the people who utter this phrase. If you don't, it is you who is the problem, and you take this very personally.

> "The year you were born marks only your entry into the world. Other years where you prove your worth, they are the ones worth celebrating."
> —*Jarod Kintz*

In this quote, *proving* your worth is critically important and worthy of celebration. Being born, evidently, is not—so forget celebrating your birthday. And what should you do in the years when you didn't happen to prove your worth? This one is especially compelling if you hold an unwanted belief that you are unworthy. Notice the subtext here: your job in life is to "prove" your worth. Implication: you, on your own, are not worthy of life; therefore, you must make up for that with the good deeds you do. If you don't accomplish good deeds, you might as well go down to the river and throw yourself off a bridge, like the Jimmy Stewart character in *It's a Wonderful Life.* Maybe, as in the film, an angel will show you how wonderful your life has been, even if it wasn't "worthy."

> "The man who thinks he can and the man who thinks he can't are both right. Which one are you?"
> —*Henry Ford*

This is the usual "think you can, and you can" pronouncement. Looks good in those glitzy posters we see on the office wall in corporate buildings, but the statement is rather asinine. Have you ever accomplished something you didn't initially think you could? If you are like most people, the answer is yes. Have you ever thought that you could do something, but as it turned out, you couldn't? The answer for most people is yes. What you may or may not have thought in the beginning, or at any other time until the end (at which time, you either have or have not accomplished your goal), is pure speculation.

Remember the bus hitting you, making crossing the street less likely? The point of this type of statement is to encourage you to adopt the claim of thinking you can, when in reality, you don't actually know. Again, we can track this back to identity. Are you this type of person, or that type of person? To further the implication, you should be this type of person, and NOT that type of person. We need to remember that some people think they are Napoleon, and think they can attack Russia with their large army, or think they are Henry Ford, and that they have invented the assembly line to mass-produce cars. These people think they can…but they are often found in mental institutions.

Speaking of Henry Ford, after his great success during the first part of his career, he was plagued with many setbacks when times changed and he did not change with them. Did he ignore reality because he was focused upon his belief that he was the *man who could*?

> "Be ashamed to die until you have won some victory for humanity."
> —*Horace Mann*

So much for freedom of choice. The assumption in this quote is that you have a job, which is to win a victory for humanity—and if you don't, shame and guilt should plague you until you have finally accomplished the prerequisite victory. Then it's okay to die. There is no appreciation for the miracle of life. Human beings are just a bunch of ants who need to contribute to the anthill.

> "You are never given a dream without also being given the power to make it true. You may have to work for it, however."
> —*Richard Bach*

This lofty-sounding platitude begins with the idea that your dreams are not of your own invention, but are given to you. Your dreams then become your marching orders from on high. The same source, it is implied, has also given you the power to manifest the dreams you are given. The "you may have to work for it, however," tells us that if we work hard, we will be able to succeed—yet many people have dreams of their own. Some of these dreams are able to be achieved, and some are not. There is nothing special about having a dream. Many of the things you want to create in your life will take work, learning, invention, steadfastness, etc., but there is no magic here, as implied in the quote. The quote also implies identity, because it is you, personally, who is given the dream and the power, and once that is in place, you have the responsibility to work for it. That is why you were given the dream in the first place. How it turns out says a lot about you.

> "As Aristotle said, 'Excellence is a habit.' I would say, furthermore, that excellence is made constant through the feeling that comes right after one has completed a work which he himself finds undeniably awe-inspiring. He only wants to relax until he's ready to renew such a feeling all over again, because to him, all else has become absolutely trivial."
> —*Criss Jami*

First of all, Aristotle was talking shop. For him, excellence was a habit, as was his intellectual integrity, penetrating mind, magnificent discipline, and understanding of specific rather than sweeping, broad notions. Aristotle would have hated what Jami made of his quote. He didn't favor generalizations. Plato said that men come and go, but humanity lives on. To Plato, humanity was the reality—less so than actual people. Aristotle disagreed. He said that collective nouns like *humanity* are convenient, but they don't actually exist in reality, and that it is actual men and women who are the true reality. Jami adds to Aristotle's observation a "return-on-investment payoff" of the emotional experience—as if the awe-inspiring work is only important because of how it makes you feel. Here, the emotional payoff is the reason one would create something great, not the thing itself. Contrast that with our Robert Frost quote: "All of the great things are done for their own sake."

"Be worthy of love, and love will come." —**Louisa May Alcott**

This is about how *worthy* of love you are…and until you are worthy, the implication is that no one will love you. If you want love, you have a job to do, which is to become worthy. This quote sounds so innocent, but it implies that people will not love you *if you are exactly the way you are.* You need to earn love, because you are not enough. It also implies a type of reciprocity. If you do your job and become worthy, then the universe will do its job and bring you a mate. Nice work if you can get it.

You can Google tens of thousands of quotes like this one, often lofty-sounding, but with built-in appeals to identity that include the things you must do in order to be a proper human being, as well as the things you shouldn't do. Almost always, the subtext is that whatever you do, it is all about *you.*

WHAT YOU SHOULD GET OUT OF THIS CHAPTER

- Some people are aware of their unwanted beliefs about themselves, and pressure themselves, through emotional conflict, *not* to be what they think they are.
- The assumption is that left to their own devices, they will do something very wrong.
- They have to be on guard against who they think they are.
- This is still about identity.
- It's not about you!

Chapter 13

IDENTITY AND PREJUDICE

THERE ARE OVER 42,000 BOOKS about race on Amazon. This chapter will not be a deep dive into one of the most complicated issues in history, as many of those books are; but issues of identity are inextricably tied to race relationships. This chapter is designed to provide insights into issues of race, identity and prejudice.

Thinking in Categories

One of the ways language works is by sorting words into class types. A word such as *chair* represents an object possessing a basic commonality with all chairs. When we say *chair*, the mind goes to the *chair* category, a grouping shared in common by all chairs. To understand the actual chair under consideration, we would begin to sort out the similarities and differences between this *particular* chair and *all* chairs. That's the way the mind works to create and use language. We have general categories of nouns (things) and verbs (actions.) We place what we see into these categories; and, once they are placed, we consider the unique differences of a particular item in contrast with the traits of the general category.

This way of thinking makes the world simple to negotiate. We don't have to rediscover the sink, the door, the TV, the car, the building, and so on. Our minds can quickly know what these objects are, and gain a sense of what is going on.

Too often, however, thinking in categories obscures accurate perception. Too often, we think we know something before we actually know it. We adopt a "this looks like that" mentality rather than observing what is before us—and because of that, we distort reality.

In 1954, psychologist Gordon Allport related prejudice to categorical thinking. Because we think in terms of generalized categories, Allport suggested that prejudice is a natural and normal process for humans. He wrote: "The human mind must think with the aid of categories. Once formed, categories are the basis for normal prejudgment. We cannot possibility avoid this process. Orderly living depends upon it."

While the mind runs on automatic, we have the added control of observation and reason. Here is the mix. There are three forces at play: *automatic categorization*, *observation*, and *reason*. In a way, sometimes they are in competition, especially when observation and reason contradict the attributes of some category the mind has generated.

It is easier to give in to the assumptions of the category than to observe more closely; and from that vantage point, use reason to come to a conclusion. It is easier to be prejudiced than not. Prejudice means you have come to conclusions BEFORE you have observed, which is completely different from true judgment, in which you reach a conclusion AFTER you have looked at facts and evidence.

You see a white person, and you think *white race* and whatever your mind attributes to that category. You see a black person, and you think *black race* and whatever your mind attributes to that category. Your mind instantly puts people into an assortment of categories. We need to understand that the mind is just doing one of its jobs. Its other jobs include observation and reason.

If you are a young, inner-city black man, you may have a category we could call *hostile police*. Whenever you see a policeman or a police car, your mind may make an automatic association of unfair treatment, danger, and antagonism. If you are a policeman working in the inner city, you may have a category we could call *gang member*. When you see a young black man, your mind may make an automatic association with life-threatening danger, violence, crime, guns, and antagonism.

These conclusions are not a product of considered thought, but instead, what seems like an instinctive survival mechanism. Each side can blame the other without considering the dynamic at play. Each side is tied to their concept of the *other*. From there, a pattern of behavior develops that reinforces each group's impression of the other. The more the police act antagonistically, the more the young black man sees the police as his enemy. The more the young black man acts antagonistically, the more the police see the young black man as their enemy. Each side will have real examples to prove their point, which entrenches their fixed concepts.

This structure leads to a destructive cycle: a policeman shoots a young, unarmed black man. He seems to get away with it. The black community protests. The protests begin peacefully, but soon, a few of the more hostile people become violent. This leads to the police feeling more defensive. Some individuals assassinate members of the police force, which reinforces to the police that they are in danger. And on it goes. Calls to reason seem weak in light of the mind's *automatic*, reactionary impulse. What makes it hard to resolve the situation is that people, unbeknownst to themselves, are players in a system: a vicious cycle fueled by the ways in which the mind categorizes.

Each side has legitimate complaints. It is true that gangs exist in the inner city, and that these gangs are dangerous. It is true that some police officers are prejudiced against black people, especially young black men. It is true that black people have a higher rate of being stopped by the police than white people. In some locations, it is five times higher. It is true that some black men are members of gangs. Most are not. The mind says *guilty before proven innocent*. The problem cannot be solved according to its own terms. What needs to happen is dominance of observation and reason over habitual categorization. Prejudice comes from mindless, automatic categorization based upon conceptual generalizations. Another way to describe this would be this: *prejudice is an example of not being in touch with reality*. Rather than seeing reality as it is, including actual risk assessment in a worst-case scenario, we generate an emotional reaction. People feel they are in danger and act defensively, with increased hostility as the cycle escalates. Each side claims that the other side is at war with them.

Tribalism

When people divide into groups, they form a type of tribe. The tribe is centered upon group identity, and membership in the tribe seems more important than individual freedom. Members are more apt to conform to the norms of the group than to follow their own sense of values and aspirations.

Tribalism is the oldest social order in the story of humanity. Like many ancient systems, tribalism existed for a good reason. Our ancestors' survival as a species depended upon it. Later in history, people began to consider their own individualism. An ongoing conflict then developed between the freedom of the individual vs. social norms and conventions.

In some countries, individualism is seen as an affront to the family and the social unit. Certain choices that one might want to make are thwarted by family identity. The pressure to uphold the identity of the family's image forces its members to live secret lives filled with hypocrisy. In these social structures, this is one of the only ways to survive.

In Kenya, Pope Francis asked a stadium filled with young people to stand up and hold hands—a simple gesture. But the deeper message was about the destructive force of tribalism, and the generative force of alignment with all of humanity. Historically, Kenya has had trouble with tribalism, even as recently as a decade ago; but tribalism is not limited to the developing world. It is a world predicament. One of the biggest issues in modern times is not terrorism, as such, but the roots of it: tribalism. The word *tribalism* has a certain primitive connotation; we think of the jungle, and people with spears running around trying to protect their area in some tropical rainforest 10,000 years ago. But in many ways, and in spite of modern civilization, tribalism, called by other names, still plagues us. Some of the other names are *nationalism*, *chauvinism*, *xenophobia*, and *intolerance*.

One of the problems in the Middle East and parts of Eastern Europe is the fact that many of the countries were created post-World War I. Within each affected country, tribalism drives prejudice, which then drives hostility, making it hard for various groups to join together in a true commonwealth.

Not all nationalism is tribalism. One can take a certain pride in the unique cultural virtues of any country: French cuisine, American rock and jazz, German engineering, Japanese design, and so on. We can share in these wonders, even if we are not members of that country. In fact, the whole world benefits from the cultural richness of many countries' unique gifts—but the ugly side of nationalism comes in the form of denouncing other groups who are not members of a certain nation (tribe.) This produces an "us against them" mentality—the notion of one group's superiority and another group's inferiority.

While issues of group identity have been with us since our earliest beginnings, the dilemma lies in the fact that they are as powerful a force now as they have ever been. And this may be a flaw of the human psyche. Our basic nature is to collect around a group of similar people. We are social animals, and seek connection with others. On one level, with the globalization of technology, this could be a good thing; people can connect with others not in their immediate "tribe." Differences enrich the larger sense of community, as people get to know each other and find that they have a lot in common. Pope Francis told his young gathering in Kenya to go online, meet others through social media, and connect with the broader world. He understood this to be an antidote to radicalization. If the whole world joins together in friendship, it is hard to become radicalized.

People who become radicalized have one thing in common: individually, they feel insecure. They, by themselves, think they are nothing—or nothing special. They seek to bolster their identities through group membership. The leaders of cults and radical movements understand this well, and are very clever at offering something these individuals lack and desperately seek: glory, glamour, and praise. It is easy to grab a gun and kill innocent people as they go about their business. It is counter-instinctive and difficult to die for such an event.

The glory, the promise of a type of stardom or rewards in heaven or paradise are compelling, but by themselves, they are not enough to overcome the instincts of survival built into the human condition. There has to be another factor to compensate for the powerful dynamic of the survival instinct—and this comes into play if the other group is not only evil, but also threatens the survival of the tribe. It is easy to unite people when they have a life-threatening enemy in common.

To accomplish this, the enemy must be seen as an existential threat. It takes ignorance of reality to buy the party line, because human beings have more in common than differences between them. Radicalism, when transposed into identity, robs culture of its richness. Everything becomes symbolic. This means that reality is not seen or understood for what it is, but becomes a symbol for what has been assigned to it. For some, it may be adopted in the name of religion, politics, or ethnic origins. It will always be about identity and tribalism.

In the West, we often hear that we need a better message to counter the messages that ISIS and al Qaeda disseminate through mastery of their propaganda machines. Given the nature of the messages, there is no counter-message that can compete. You can't fight one appeal to group identity with a different appeal to group identity. The basic premise of identity itself needs to be revealed as the charade it is.

A more sophisticated social structure would involve freedom of the individual within the context of a healthy and productive community. This is more complex to manage. It requires more than a mere tolerance of differences; it also demands an appreciation of differences. It calls for the deep human desire to join together with others to build something we cannot do on our own. Such a structure brings out the best in everyone—not as some utopian ideal, but as a highly workable social order which itself represents an invention of humanity, well beyond a tribal mindset. Pope Francis understood this well when he asked people of all nations, beliefs, ethnic groups, and cultures to join hands in an act of common humanity.

Dark Girls

The 2013 Oscar winner for best supporting actress was Lupita Nyong'o, for her extraordinary portrayal of the tortured slave Patsey in Steve McQueen's *12 Years A Slave.* A few days before the Academy Awards ceremonies, Nyong'o accepted the award for Best Breakthrough Performance at the seventh-annual Black Women in Hollywood Luncheon hosted by *Essence* magazine.

She talked about having a dark complexion. This was not an actual reference to race, but to color. Nyong'o's complexion is very dark. From the time she was a child, she thought there was something wrong with being dark. She never thought she was beautiful because of her color, and secretly wished for lighter skin. Nyong'o said she tried to make a deal with God; that she would no longer lose her school sweater, and she would obey her mother, if she could just have lighter skin. She would wake up in the morning, rush to her mirror, and find there had been no change of color. After years of this, she said, "I had begun to enjoy the seduction of inadequacy."

Her confession hit something deeply understood by the other women in the room, many of whom were in tears as they witnessed this extraordinarily talented and beautiful woman disclosing something they all knew: the identity of color. That very same month, Nyong'o was on the cover of the most glamorous magazine in the world: *Vogue*.

Ironically, prejudice about the darkness of one's skin is found mostly among people of the same race. Shade becomes a factor of identity, and the underlying prejudice is that lighter is better—and darker is worse. In a revealing documentary entitled *Dark Girls* by Bill Duke and D. Channsin Berry, the camera exposes an ugly truth: color prejudice, now termed *colorism*. In one heartbreaking scene, a little black girl is shown a series of images of a cartoon girl. From left to right, the very same girl's image becomes darker, until the furthest-right picture is very dark. The little girl is asked to point to the girl who is smartest. Her finger quickly moves to the image further to the left—the whitest one. Then she is asked who is the least smart. Her finger quickly points to the darkest image, on the right. Who is the nicest person? The white image. Who is the meanest? The darkest image. This is a version of an experiment conducted in the 1940s by Kenneth and Marmie Clark which demonstrated that black children carried internalized racism. Asked to select a doll, the children most often chose a light-skinned doll over a dark-skinned doll.

In one scene in the film, a woman describes a time when she was fourteen years old and riding in the back of her family's car. Her mother said, "She is very smart and very pretty." Had her comments stopped there, the girl would have been very pleased, but her mother went on to say, "If only she were two shades lighter." This last remark was crushing to the girl, and, from that time to adulthood, she thought there was something wrong with the color of her skin.

Where do these prejudices come from? Of course, history is filled with the chronicle of white domination over people of color. A prime example of this, prominent during the heyday of the British Empire, was termed the "white man's burden." The institution of slavery was a direct manifestation of the dehumanization of people of color, so as to enslave them while continuing to claim "Christian" values. At the time, the "fact" was obvious to everyone that white people succeeded, and darker-colored people were dependent upon them. Of course, there are so many aspects to consider in understanding this dynamic; this brief description doesn't do justice to the grand sweep of history behind the color factor of identity. The results of this history, however, are all too easy to see in current hiring practices, educational opportunities, social fairness, and issues of equality—and, of course, in our justice system.

Within a single group identity, there exist various subdivisions that function to position people in hierarchies. Concepts like *I'm better than you because I belong to this or that subdivision* plague the human condition to the point where basic humanity is lost. One's group is seen as the determining factor in life. To counter racial prejudice, the slogan *black is beautiful* was invented; and while there is now an exceedingly positive slant on what it means to be black, the focus is still on identity. Positive or negative, identity is about focus upon the self: who you are, and who you are in relation to other people, groups, or subgroups.

In reality, we are who we are: human beings. Human beings exist in many racial forms. There isn't a good race and a bad race—but people will pretend there is. Sometimes, this is subtle. Generalizations come easily, but we won't dignify the ones that paint entire groups of people with the same broad, negative brushstroke. If these attitudes are taught to children, an undercurrent of bias reaches through the years and well into adulthood. Often, however, these prejudices exist in direct conflict with people's own deepest values. If one of your values is that all people should have an equal chance in life, but at the same time, you carry a built-in prejudice, that prejudice will be hard to see, hard to admit, hard to observe, hard to talk about, and hard to address.

Identity is made to seem important, when in reality, it is unimportant. This doesn't mean, however, that the *world* thinks it is unimportant—but in this case, the world is wrong. IN REALITY, identity is unimportant. If you exist as a human being, you will be a member of one group or another, and since no group is better or worse than any other, what does identity have to do with anything? There exists no group lacking examples of great geniuses, artists, inventors, humanitarians, doctors, teachers, and citizens. As the great Arthur Ashe once said, "My potential is more than can be expressed within the bounds of my race or ethnic identity."

Welcome to the Orchestra

One example of a field in which talent and ability should be the only standard for hiring is the symphony orchestra, yet over the years, more white men than women and/or minorities have had an edge in filling these much-coveted positions. Was this a factor of unconscious prejudice? Perhaps, because a new practice was developed to create a level playing field: the blind audition. Many major orchestras have adopted the practice of having musicians audition behind curtains so they cannot be seen. Therefore, they can only be judged on their playing. The result: more women and minorities get jobs.

Categorizing by Style

When Robert's wife first came to America from her native England, she went shopping in a fairly up-market shop in Boston. She was dressed very nicely, and received first-class service: respectful, helpful, friendly. A few days later she went back to the very same store, but this time, she was wearing jeans and a casual top. She was the same person, in the same store, and she spoke with the same beautiful English accent—but this time, she was not treated well at all. Some of the same salespeople, who evidently did not recognize her from her previous visit, were rude, dismissive, and discourteous.

They must have categorized her by the clothes she was wearing, writing off a customer who was dressed informally. That, of course, is simply stupid business, but it demonstrates some of the dimensions of prejudice on a subtler level.

Without knowing the actual people, the mind can come to false conclusions based upon its mechanism of putting everything into fixed categories: rich, poor, white, black, Latino, Asian, African, South American, and so on.

How Doctors Think

In Jerome Groopman's book, *How Doctors Think*, he points out that the many of the misdiagnoses doctors make are based upon their quick conclusions about the patient. He says that this often happens within the first 18 seconds of the visit. Because the doctor has an automatic prejudice about the patient, he or she decides about the credibility of their complaints. Too often, this leads to catastrophic results. It represents another example of the mind automatically categorizing people based upon how they look.

Doctors have been trained to observe and reason to a greater extent than most people, but the traditional medical model is to diagnose and prescribe treatment. The method is based upon categorization of symptoms, followed by common practice therapies. This is a good process, in general, because it places knowledge into an accessible system; and most often, doctors are correct in their diagnoses. Yet even with such a good system, human error arising from prejudice can cause doctors to fall short. Far too often, this type of error is seen in the case of morbidly obese patients. Overweight patients overwhelmingly report being treated disrespectfully by health professionals because of their weight. One study found that 53% of overweight and obese women reported receiving inappropriate comments about their weight from their doctors. Obese patients who report perceptions of weight discrimination avoid seeking routine preventive care, such as cancer screenings.

Even if doctors don't directly express weight-based judgments, their biases can hurt patients. One recent study showed that the higher a patient's body mass, the less respect doctors express for that patient. And the less respect a doctor has for a patient, says Dr. Mary Huizinga, the study's lead author and an assistant professor at the Johns Hopkins School of Medicine, the less time the doctor spends with the patient—and the less information he or she offers.

Ignorance

Professor Stuart Firestein, neuroscientist and chairman of the Department of Biology at Columbia University, in his book *Ignorance—How It Drives Science*, writes that most people have a false impression of science. Rather than what most of us learned in school as the "scientific method," Firestein says, "…it's mostly a tale woven by newspaper reports, television documentaries, and high-school lesson plans." He goes on to describe the true scientific process as the pursuit of an understanding of the unknown. In fact, he created a course entitled

Ignorance, in which guest scientists speak for a few hours about what they don't know. Rather than rely upon categorization, the students learn how to better observe and reason. As Sir Isaac Newton said, "Hypotheses has no place in science." Similarly, Rene Descartes said, "To understand any set of phenomena, first rid yourself of preconceptions."

Knowing that the mind mechanistically puts things into preconceived categories, the most creative scientists discipline their thought processes so as to observe objectively and without prejudice. This is not always easy to do, as the needed skills may take years to develop. Mathematics helps, because it is a truly structural language.

In Walter Isaacson's excellent biography, *Einstein: His Life and Universe*, he writes that one of Einstein's unique qualities was that he was not rooted in the past. He could, as Descartes instructed, rid himself of all preconceptions. In Einstein's case, that included all of Newtonian physics.

While it may seem impossible for average people to "rid themselves of all preconceptions," there are, in fact, some fields in which this feat is a built-in skill. One of them is accounting. An accountant must look at the actual numbers under consideration. Of course, accountants know what to do with the numbers once they have been considered, but at the same time, they do not think in generalized concepts. They never say to their clients, "You know, you look a lot like the fellow who was in last week. He only had to pay $4,030 in tax. I'm sure if you send $4,030 to the tax man, he'll be happy." If you don't rid yourself of all preconceptions in the field of accounting, you could end up in jail!

Identity and Prejudice

It is one thing to hold a concept that your mind assumes to be true. It is quite another to hold a concept that is inherently tied to your identity. Observation and reason can overturn an inaccurate concept, but it takes more than that when identity is tied to the concept. Sometimes, no amount of objective fact and evidence can change the concept. The reason for this is that anything that contradicts the concept seems like a personal attack, or a threat to one's existence. This is because some concepts and beliefs are tied to a person's identity. Of course, as we have said before, you are not your beliefs or concepts. This understanding may help to overcome feelings of threat when a deeply-held belief or concept is challenged.

Beliefs about others, especially groups, can also become fixed, as if those ideas are inextricably tied to your own identity. The older you get, the more the tendency leads to getting fixed in your ways. Once you settle into a worldview, it becomes harder and harder to change your mind. Your mind can become entrenched in rigid, inflexible, unyielding concepts that are resistant to change, defying logic and good sense. This is not a good pattern. Age alone doesn't cause this, for many of the world's most creative people have become more and more flexible and open as they have gotten older.

Knowing how the mind works—that it is more apt to automatically jump to conclusions based upon prejudice—places special focus upon observation and reason. This is a discipline one can develop over time, and with practice.

WHAT YOU SHOULD GET OUT OF THIS CHAPTER

- Prejudice comes, in part, from the mind's function of putting things into categories.
- This is automatic.
- The mind can also observe and reason.
- Too often, the mind's automatic process of categorization misses reality.
- The discipline of observation and reason can correct this tendency.
- When personal identity is tied to group identity, people can separate into a form of tribalism.
- There are two forms of nationalism: cultural enrichment and division.
- No one race is better than any other.
- All human beings will belong to some sort of group. What they all have in common is their humanity.
- Prejudice distorts reality.
- As we get older, we can either become more rigid or more flexible.

Chapter 14

HOW YOUR IDENTITY MAY BE WEIGHING YOU DOWN

Obesity is a global epidemic with a profound effect on the health of the worldwide population; and as fellow human, if you are not personally struggling with your weight, you are likely surrounded with loved ones, friends, and colleagues who are. The United States tops the list of the most obese countries in the world (in terms of total number of citizens affected), followed by China, India, Russia, Brazil, Mexico, Egypt, Germany, Pakistan, and Indonesia. Over two-thirds of people living in the U.S. and Mexico, as well as a great percentage of individuals around the world who are exposed to the American way of life, suffer with ongoing weight challenges. And most, despite knowing what they *ought* to do to improve their health, just can't seem to get the job done.

We understand that this public health issue is influenced by a spectrum of individual-level, social-network, and environmental factors. Individual factors such as unhealthy diet, excessive calorie intake, inactivity, inadequate sleep, excessive stress, older age, smoking cessation, and genetics play into each person's susceptibility to weight gain. As a social disease, family eating and activity habits, close friends' behaviors, and other lifestyle factors can heavily influence a person's weight! If you spend time with obese people, you are more likely to become obese, as published in a landmark 2007 paper in *The New England Journal of Medicine* by Nicholas A. Christakis and James H. Fowler, entitled "The Spread of Obesity in a Large Social Network over 32 Years."

Environmental influences, including access to walking, exercise, and healthy food, are critical, but are typically lacking in lower-socioeconomic, inner-city environments. Our work leads us to observe that too often, the issue of identity contributes to the inability of those struggling with their weight to make any sustainable change, no matter how hard they try.

The current approach taken by most people is to go on a diet. As we have mentioned previously, as many as 85% of people who go on a diet with the intention of losing weight gain the weight back within two years. Unfortunately, not only is the current approach simply ineffective—many times, the diet actually results in the dieter ending up heavier than they were before they attempted to lose weight.

You might notice that this sounds like an oscillating pattern. Yep—you're right! And while physiological factors are involved in the pattern, the structural dynamics are predominant. Often, a sound approach to weight loss is not sustainable—because the person's underlying structure does not support it, and because it includes the element of identity. For most people, the way they see themselves represents a complicating factor in the successful pursuit of a healthy weight.

The Notion That Your Weight Issues Make You Less

Let's explore the impact that identity can have, first on the reinforcement of obesity, then upon the ways in which identity can thwart the efforts of an individual to sustain weight loss.

Our childhoods are impacted and influenced by many factors, including genetics, our family's lifestyle, our school, and other environmental and psychosocial factors. During early development, if you feel like you don't belong, or are in trouble with your peers and the adults in your life—and feel the powerlessness of childhood, as well—you may overeat, just to compensate for the emotional conflict you experience. Overeating is a type of self-soothing used to reduce the anxiety you feel, as well as a substitution for something you may be missing. Food can be used to make up for the lack of an empathetic caregiver, on the one hand, or an over-empathetic caregiver who overfeeds the entire family in an attempt to demonstrate love and caring, on the other. This often leads to obesity, but what happens next drives identity issues even deeper. As a developing child, you are in danger of being ostracized by family and friends during a very influential part of your maturation. You become stigmatized by those closest to you. You feel separate, not as good as others, and as if something is very wrong with you.

Let's look at some of the research supporting the various ways in which our social connections can contribute to the creation of a belief that somehow, people who are obese somehow do not measure up. There exists a body of research that presents evidence about obese children actually being treated differently, with less respect and consideration. In a study published in 2010 in *Obesity*, researchers from the University of North Texas reported that parents of obese offspring were less likely to chip in and help their overweight child buy a car. "It may have been a result of greater strain in those relationships," responded Dan Kirshenbaum, author and professor at Northwestern.

In contrast, Mike Bishop, the executive director of Wellspring, a boarding school for weight loss, said, "Parents of obese children tended to be *helicopter* parents—overinvolved in their life and a little but too caring, kind of killing them with kindness, which is how they got that way in the first place."

The tendency of parents to treat their kids differently encourages obese children to think that there is something different about (or even wrong with) them.

Early Peer Groups, a new study out of the University of Leeds, points out that children as young as four years of age have internalized the idea that *overweight* means *bad.* Researchers spoke with 126 children between the age of four and seven years old. Each child read a picture book featuring a character named Alfie (a little boy,) or Alfina (a little girl), who, in different versions of the story, was a normal weight, overweight, or in a wheelchair. Only one of the 43 children who heard the overweight version of the story said they would befriend him or her. Additionally, they rated the overweight version as less likely to get invited to parties, to be happy with his or her looks, to win a race, or to excel in school (more so than those in a wheelchair.) This represents more evidence confirming a huge social awareness of body size, as well as prejudice against obesity.

When interviewed, Professor Andrew Hill, one of the study's authors, said that the children's gender did not impact their feelings, though older subjects were more likely to have a greater fat prejudice. "I think we have an underlying social commentary about weight and morals, and that the morality of people is based on their shape," he said. "I think that is very powerful, and kids are sensitive to it."

The evidence is building that young kids internalize stereotypes and negative feelings about fat. A 2010 study found that three- to five-year-old girls were more likely to choose a thin or average-sized Candyland® piece than a fat one, making disparaging statements about the rejected piece, like "She is fat. I don't want to be that one." Not only do children express prejudice toward others, they turn these prejudices onto themselves, not wanting to be what they think they are. The reality is that we live in a world where three-, five-, and seven-year-olds are terrified of being branded as "fat." Dickinson College professor Amy Farrell, author of *Fat Shame: Stigma and the Fat Body in American Culture*, told CNN, "Fat prejudice is such a strong cultural idea that children are going to start picking up on it immediately."

This external differentiation continues into *college* and into the *workplace*. A recent study by the Center for Creative Leadership found that top managers with a high body mass index were judged more harshly and seen as less effective than their slimmer colleagues by their peers, both at work and in the context of interpersonal relationships. Studies have documented that overweight adults often don't fare as well at work, in school, and in love. They are also less likely to complete high school, enter and finish college, or get married; additionally, they are more likely to be poor.

The existing research and our own experience working with individuals have shown that it is not uncommon for people who are struggling with their weight to hold significant unwanted beliefs concerning themselves. This makes losing weight seem like a personal identity struggle rather than an objective process of applying the right methods and adopting the right habits. Obese people often have one of three compensatory strategies.

First, they may be in complete denial, thinking they do not have limitations related to obesity, or that their weight will not prevent them from creating their life-building process. Since they are denying reality, they are unable to have much of an impact upon the improvement of their health.

Second, they may have just plain given up, feeling that their ability to change the condition is hopeless. They might think they are victims, and blame others, themselves, their conditions, fate, and their environment.

Or third, they are actively focusing upon losing weight, in the contemplative, decision-making, or in-action phase, hopeful that this time, it will *actually work*.

A recent study by Markus Schafer, from the Center on Aging and the Life Course at Purdue University, confirmed that obesity not only represents a health risk, but also places the individual at a disadvantaged social position. In addition, weight discrimination exacerbates actual health risks and functional disability. This means that people who are obese become more focused upon how others see them—which, in turn, increases their stress and exerts an additional negative impact upon their health and how functional they are.

In addition, our life satisfaction is related to the weight of the people around us. In a paper titled *Obesity (Sometimes) Matters* from the University of Colorado, obese people were much less happy if they lived in an area where very few people were obese. In other words, rating our life satisfaction is based upon the degree to which we compare with everyone else. If you are obese or even overweight, you might be thinking, "Okay, the deck is stacked against me!"

What to do? Here is just ONE basic question to answer:

Do you want to be optimally healthy?

If the answer is YES, then we have one critical piece of advice:

Get the attention off of yourself and onto your life-building process!

We know it can feel awfully personal, to be overweight. After all, no one forced you to eat. You were not tied to a chair with people shoving food down your throat. It was you who ordered the food at the restaurant, filled your plate at the buffet, and had the midnight snack. Yet those behaviors, like all behaviors, were caused by an underlying structure. The key to successfully changing the picture begins with a change of focus: away from you, and toward *creating what matters most to you*. If you are trying to adopt a new, healthy habit, but your focus is on *you*, you will find it hard to learn. You will make missteps and mistakes—all of which come with changing your lifestyle.

Not only will you need to get the focus off of yourself and onto the health outcome you want to achieve, you will also need to ignore what other people think of you. They don't get a vote. As in any major life change, not everyone wants to see you succeed. For some, it represents a threat to their claims of powerlessness, and to their ability to do what they want if you're off doing what you want. Remember, there are two patterns generated by structure: *oscillating* and *advancing*. You want to move from oscillation to advancement.

Once you move to an advancing structure, your motivation is clear and simple: better health and optimal well-being.

Focusing upon this desired outcome, along with your current reality (structural tension), will enable you to make the daily, secondary choices that are needed in order to support the building of habits that lead to health and well-being.

How you feel about yourself, and how well or poorly you may have done each day, will no longer matter. All that will matter will be steady progress: getting a little better at eating, moving, sleeping, and handling stress. And you will build resolve as a result of the learning, practicing, supporting, modeling, and the small choices that support what is most important to you.

Shirley Mast, a registered nurse, lost over 200 pounds and progressively created better health and well-being over a period of five years by shifting her focus away from what she *thought* about herself and onto what she *wanted* for herself. Of course, that's not all she did. She completely changed her lifestyle habits; but her change of underlying structure enabled her to first reach a healthy weight, and then maintain it over the years. Here is what she reported:

> *Prior to taking the steps to get healthy, I'd resigned myself to living my remaining few years trapped by morbid obesity. I simply didn't think it was possible to escape from what had become my reality. In fact, I had started making scrapbooks to leave for my unborn grandkids, since I knew I would never see them. Even when I started my journey to health, I did it with the idea that perhaps I could lose 25 pounds or so, and possibly avoid a very premature death. I didn't believe that a complete and total health transformation was possible.*

Fortunately, I soon discovered that I truly could effectively improve my health in a dramatic way, and my orientation shifted completely. Instead of defining myself by who I had become and making my life choices based on what I thought was probable, I started looking at what I could create in my life if anything were possible. My desire to be optimally healthy has moved my mindset from accepting what is probable to creating what is possible, and has inspired even more creativity for me. When I took my identity — who I thought I was — out of the equation, and implemented small steps to help me move towards optimal health, a seemingly endless horizon of opportunities opened for me. And oh, by the way, I am now babysitting my grandchild, and I am more than 200 pounds lighter."

—Shirley Mast, R.N.

In the past, Shirley had tried to lose weight. She yo-yoed several times in the cycle, losing weight only to put it back on. This time, it was different. Let's analyze what changed between her trying to lose weight—dieting almost constantly, and focusing upon all the limits she had in her life—to the ability to lose and then sustain a healthy and dramatically different lifestyle.

For most of her life, she not only knew she needed to lose weight in order to feel better, but as a nurse, she knew all of the things to be worried about, such as heart disease, stroke, diabetes, and cancer, to name a few threats. She would worry herself into action because she felt so much emotional conflict. In fact, the last time she had gone on a diet came as a direct result of thinking she was going to die.

Negative consequences were the driving motivation, and, as we explored in Chapter 11—The Marshmallow Test, behavior like this produces a predictable oscillating pattern.

Let's look at Shirley's previous motivation and behavior, and why it did not result in sustainable change.

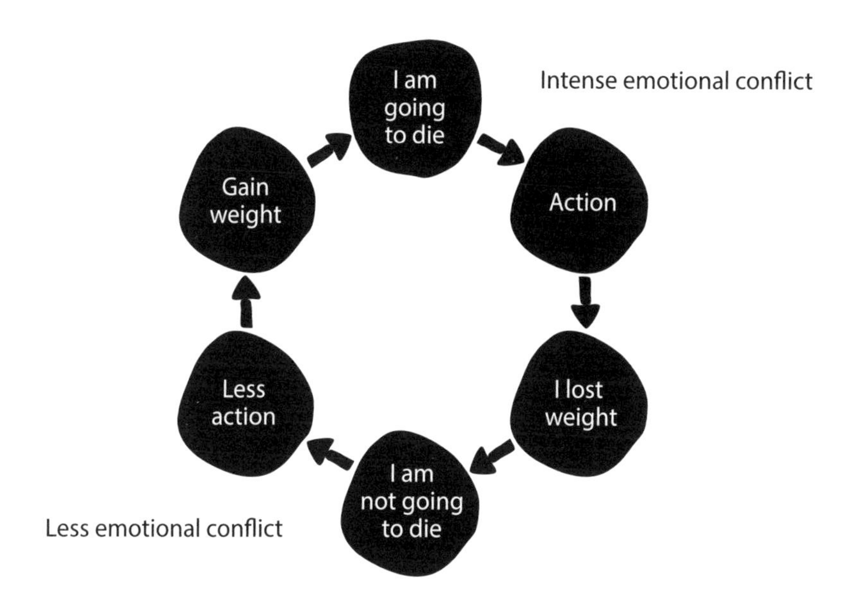

Shirley's emotionally driven motivation lost its power once she lost a few pounds. Then she no longer felt the same level of emotional conflict that had been driving the action in the first place. Less conflict, and perhaps less guilt or fear, reduced her sense of urgency. Less conflict, however, also led to a return to her old habits, setting up a vicious new cycle of dieting.

Now that Shirley has taken her identity out of the structure, she can more easily keep her focus on what matters to her, which is to create optimal health and well-being. She can be honest with herself about the current reality, as the new structure in her life *is structural tension.*

We can see a very different pattern:

Primary Choice		Optimal Health
Secondary Choices	Habits of Health Weight Loss	
	Habits of Healthy Eating	
	Habits of Healthy Motion	
	Habits of Healthy Sleep	
	Habits of Stress Reduction	
		Current Reality

Before and After

Over the last decades, we have seen countless stories of people like Shirley who changed their lifestyle, but were unable to do it through conflict or willpower manipulation. They had to be clear about the outcome they wanted, reality as it actually existed in relationship to their goal, and a strategic plan that turned good intentions into action—AND a refocus from identity to a life-building process.

WHAT YOU SHOULD GET OUT OF THIS CHAPTER

- When identity is tied to obesity, it is harder to create better health.
- When you get the attention off of yourself and onto the health outcome you want to create, you increase your possibilities of success.

Chapter 15

ADVERTISING AND IMAGE: QUESTIONS OF IDENTITY

IN ONE RADIO AD for Rosetta Stone®, the narrator tells us that we won't be a better person if we buy that new pair of shoes or a 40-inch flat-screen TV—but if we learned a foreign language, well then…

An ad for Mass Mutual® says, "Who you love says a lot about you."

The advertising industry wants to sell you things—after all, that is their job. No problem with that. But over the decades, the focus in the field has shifted away from the company's products and services toward you, the consumer, and your identity. From a scholarly paper entitled *Mirrors of Masculinity: Representation and Identity in Advertising Images* by Jonathan E. Schroeder and Detlev Zwick, the authors write:

> "Many contemporary ads make little mention of the advertised product or service. Visual arrangements

are such that the advertised good often drops into the background while highly abstract connections are made between the models, a lifestyle and the brand. Viewers are asked to transfer meaning from the look of the people in the ad—their image, lifestyle, and physical appearance—onto the product.

"...Sociologist Erving Goffman pointed out that ads impact directly on lived experience by normatively limiting our conceptions of identity, right and wrong, and the good life. Critically, ads influence how we think about masculinity and femininity, what is sexy, and what will be seen as attractive by others.

"Goffman showed that 'every physical surround, every box for social gatherings, necessarily provides materials than can be used in the display of gender and the affirmation of gender identity.' Standard advertising poses generally signal men's dominance over submissive women, be it through physical, financial, or psychological superiority. By focusing upon behavior as performance, he challenged the distinction between the image and lived experience.

"Our group helps form our identity, and often, the stronger appeal is to our identity rather than our individual self-interest....You can make an emotional appeal to people's identity even when an appeal to self-interest doesn't work."

That is an astonishing statement. Appeals to identity are more powerful than what is in our own best interest. A good example of this can be found in the famous Marlboro Man® cigarette commercial. He was a cowboy: tall, strong, and independent, the alter-ego of Clint Eastwood. He had a very cool cowboy hat, and rugged skin from being out in the elements day after day. The fact that he was killing himself with cigarettes didn't matter. He looked great as he lit up, taking in a big drag, holding it in his lungs for a moment, and then blowing out the coolest cloud of blue smoke to highlight his cowboy features. Sadly, the actor who played the Marlboro Man died of lung cancer. Of course, he was an actor playing a part; the Marlboro Man is a fantasy on the same level as Mickey Mouse or the fabulous-looking models on the cover of *Cosmo*.

The Look

Today, slick lifestyle magazines feature page after page of ads for the major brands: Louis Vuitton, Prada, MaxMara, Hermès, Yves Saint Laurent, Hugo Boss, Dior, and countless others. The thing is, there seems to be something strange going on. It seems that if you wear these expensive designer clothes, you can't be happy. All of the models are sad, serious, angry at something, or simply depressed. All of them are young, beautiful, and pouty. Attitude, maybe? Sex appeal? Dedicated to research, we took one magazine and counted the sets of Bridget Bardot-style front teeth. Twenty-eight of the ladies in the magazine had them—maybe more, but the others had their mouths closed. The men were also experiencing a bad day in their designer clothes. They looked off into the distance, or just down. One or two looked at the camera with pronounced disdain, as if to say, "Who are you to look at me wearing these clothes?"

Maybe that's good marketing. It must be, since they all have *the look*. Okay, we get it. It's cool to look unhappy, depressed, distant, annoyed, bored, serious, or miserable. These models are total professionals. They all can do it. Amazing! Think about the hours of practice in front of their mirrors, the hours of pouting, not unlike a pianist's dedication to practicing scales to use when performing Mozart. What do amateurs do when in front of a camera?

We all have our own unique look. Notice that all of the pictures you are in have that same "picture smile" you always use. If you look through pictures taken over a twenty-year period, you will notice that everyone, in every picture, had their own same smile. Year after year, no matter what was really going on in life, there it was: the look. But of course, that look was not THE look, the one the pros have.

Both looks are fiction—that is to say, we are putting on a show. We are actors for the moment. We are creating something, making a presentation. And that's fine, and often fun, as long as we understand that it is fiction, something made-up, and not really us at all. It's not really the models at all, either. I'll bet that in their family snapshots, they have their own goofy picture smile. If not, then in the family snapshot of the holiday celebration, there would be all of these smiling people, and one with THE look on his or her face. What will their kids say, 20 years from now, at just the age when kids love to laugh at their parents' fashion choices? "Hey, Mom, how come you have that look on your face? Did you get food poisoning that day?"

"It's hard to explain," comes the answer that doesn't really explain that they were in training to be a professional model.

The essence of the creative process is to create something that didn't exist before we created it. We bring something into being. It could be fiction, like a story; or a play, a poem, a song, a film, or a book. It could be something more: the life you want to live. In *that* creative process, reality is needed rather than fiction. The life we want to create is not a picture-smile or a pouty frown for the sake of the camera. It is something we end up living. To create this, one needs to go beyond posing or presenting an identity, to others or to oneself. Too often, people are posing for their mental cameras. They want to look a certain way; but in the creative process, especially when the subject is your life itself, there is no room for posing, no room for identity issues. You need to see everything exactly as it really is—warts and all.

Just Add an Egg

In 1952, Betty Crocker introduced a new, easy-to-make cake mix. All you needed to do was add water, stir, and bake. The strategic product direction for the company was to create goods that were almost effortless to make—for example, Bisquick®, for which the slogan was "90 seconds from package to oven." Bisquick® was "invented" in 1930 after one of their sales executives, traveling in a train dining car, complimented the railroad chef on his outstanding fresh biscuits. The chef told him his secret—that he had made a pre-mixed batter consisting of lard, flour, baking powder, and salt. All he had to do was put it in a baking pan and bake. Back home at the corporation, the executive replicated the chef's idea of a mixture that was ready to go right into the oven, and created Bisquick®. The product hit the shelves in 1931, and it was an instant sensation.

General Mills thought that the instant cake mix would also be an instant hit, but to their surprise, sales were slow. The company engaged two business psychologists, Dr. Burleigh Gardner and Dr. Ernet Dichter. Their studies found that housewives felt guilty about making a cake so easily. Somehow, it went against their notion of what it was to be a good 1950s housewife, so the psychologists suggested one additional step in the process: the housewife would add one egg to the mixture. The mixture didn't need them to add an egg in order for it to work, but putting in that additional direction caused women to feel that they were doing their job. Of course, the egg was really symbolic of their identity as good wives and mothers. Ease and convenience were important, but not if they got in the way of housewives' image of themselves.

This little story contains a world of insight. If the 1950s housewife had been focused upon creating a satisfactory outcome in the most convenient way, simply adding water to the mix would have been fine. How many other extra steps or symbolic gestures do we add, just to bolster our identity? Often, the symptoms of identity issues are found in small, almost invisible acts.

For many people, if success comes too easily, they can't handle it, and think they didn't earn it. With that dynamic in place, the pattern is for the person to manage to screw up his or her success over time. Often, people feel better about themselves having failed than having succeeded, if the success came too easily. They are equating success or failure with the degree to which they thought they did or didn't earn the success.

You want something; that is the outcome. If it came to you in some miraculous way, or if you had to work your fingers to the bone, what difference would it make? Some people have more talent than others. Talent only means that some skill or mentality comes easily. People with less talent, but the same goals, must work much harder in order to accomplish similar results. It would be nice if we could just snap our fingers and have more talent and natural ability, but the fact is, we only have as much as we have. That is the starting point…but not the ending point.

Commonly, people who end up accomplishing astonishing results do so *because* of their lack of natural ability—they have to work a bit harder than more talented people. This says nothing about the person. The dedication to creating the result matters. The process will be as easy or hard as it has to be. While people love to glorify process, it matters little. To Mozart, music came easily. It seemed to pour out of his imaginative mind. For Beethoven, music didn't pour freely from his mind. He worked it over and over, testing, experimenting, developing, growing, and deepening his artistic abilities. Both men produced some of the greatest music ever written—but what if Mozart had been affected by an identity issue that caused him to think that his music came to him too easily, and therefore couldn't be very good? Or what if Beethoven thought if he didn't have the talent of a Mozart, he should give up trying to compose? Of course, it's easy to see the absurdity of the concept when it comes to Mozart or Beethoven, but when this concept strikes closer to home, it is taken more seriously.

Here is a theme to understand throughout your own life: *what you think about yourself doesn't matter a bit in the creative process.* You don't need to add an egg when it is not needed just to pander to your identity issues, if you happen to have any. Use the egg example to see if there are other ways you are creating false symbols to prove to yourself that you have earned your success. If you have talent, nice. If you don't have talent for the things you want to do—also nice. Just a different menu. Remember the Mozart/Beethoven lesson, and carry on.

WHAT YOU SHOULD GET OUT OF THIS CHAPTER

- Advertisers try to make their ads a matter of identity. You are wonderful if you use their products.
- Therefore, they hope you will base your buying decision upon how you see yourself rather than the value and worth of their product.
- For some housewives in the 1950s, if the mix was too easy, they thought they were not living up to the ideal they held for themselves.
- Business psychologists found that if they added an egg, the housewives would feel as if they were doing their job.
- You don't need to "add an egg" when it is not needed, simply to pander to your identity issues.
- What you think about yourself is irrelevant to the creative process.

Chapter 16

THE INDIVIDUAL AND SOCIETY

Benjamin Franklin wisely said, "Man is a social animal, and it is punishment to live alone."

Studies show that prisoners who spend excessive time in solitary confinement experience harmful psychological effects that can produce debilitating symptoms such as visual and auditory hallucinations, hypersensitivity, paranoia, uncontrollable rage, fear, distortions of time and perception, and post-traumatic stress disorder. The United Nations Convention Against Torture has condemned the use of solitary confinement as torture.

We don't like to be alone for too long. We need to connect with other people, or we can lose our grip on reality. We are, as Franklin observed, social animals, and therein lies the age-old dilemma, for most people: how to be members of a social structure without losing one's soul.

On the one hand, in order to be part of society, we must conform to certain behaviors and practices. We are expected to have good manners, avoid hurting others, follow traffic laws, abide by the norms, bathe or shower regularly, and dress in ways that are socially acceptable.

On the other hand, we want to express our individualism. There exists a healthy instinct in human nature to rebel against conformity, to go against the tide, to be independent and free, to make one's own decisions.

Most people have trouble finding the right balance between conformity and individualism. Throw in an identity issue here or there, and you're headed for a *social* existential crisis. *Who am I* leads to *who am I in society*? When that's the case, you can begin to define yourself in relation to your status. For some, self-concept is inextricably tied to social class, economic standing, career position, and/or reputation in the community. If you are defining yourself according to your position in the social structure, you will always be insecure. This is the famous "keeping up with the Joneses" mentality. If someone in your social class gets a better washing machine, you have to get one, too. If they get a boat, you'll need to get one. If they have a 50-inch TV screen, you'd better start shopping around. If they have the latest iPhone, even if the one you have is perfectly fine, it's off to the computer store.

Many who make it to the "top of the heap" confuse themselves with their position. They can become intoxicated with power and attention. Public praise can be addictive, and it can also distort one's sense of reality. This leads people to make some very bad decisions, ones that often end in public ridicule.

Often, over time, people lose their social position. This is commonly referred to as "a fall from grace." For people in the public eye, this change can be a hard one to take. Robert Frost wrote in his poem, *Provide*:

No memory of having starred
Atones for later disregard
Or keeps the end from being hard.

Identity issues are just as prevalent on the other side of the socioeconomic scale—though here, identity takes on the image of oppression, prejudice, or the experience of being downtrodden. It also takes on a counter-cultural contrast: street culture or ghetto culture. When channeled into art, something very creative can happen. New forms of music, dance, and even visual art come from the inner city rather than universities. Artistic productions notwithstanding, issues of identity become a badge of honor designed to compensate for feelings of inadequacy and insecurity.

Groups that have been marginalized often create a compensating strategy that takes pride in what has been rejected. Black power, feminism, gay pride, and other such movements all had their origins in the repression and subjugation of the group. The group forms a subculture, and counters its social rejection by affirming pride in what has been criticized. From this, positive social change can take place, as people become able to rethink the deeper issues that divide people. Over time, the new version of pride becomes assimilated into the social norm, and no longer holds a unique purpose. That is why many of these movements fade over time. It is not because they have accomplished all of their goals, but because the group is no longer marginalized. Often, people lose themselves in a group—because their identity comes from the group, not from themselves as individuals. They see themselves as the Hell's Angels, or Gay Pride Day, or Black Lives Matter rather than Sam, Judy, Leon, or Tyler. They become unable to separate themselves from the group, and lose their sense of individuality.

Alone and Together

Here is a statement that may at first seem contradictory: *Freedom of the individual is made available by being separate from others, while at the same time together with others.* Even though this idea can seem a little hard to fully grasp, once you understand the principle, it will make a new experience of human interaction available to you.

Too often, people lose themselves when they are with others. Their own sense of self seems to disappear. After a long day of being with people, you may hear some say, "I'm peopled out." They need to be alone to recharge their batteries. If this is a familiar experience for you, then this section of the book will be especially important.

Step one in developing this principle is to learn how to be alone. This may sound simple, but it is not as easy as it might seem. Most people have trouble being alone with themselves. They may not be in the company of other people, but they are hardly alone. They watch TV, listen to music, read, play video games, text, surf the web, cook, and fill their minds with other distractions.

Over the years, we have discovered one of the major reasons people exhibit this behavior; and the next section will explore this. In one of the Robert Fritz workshops, participants were asked to sit opposite another person. The direction was very clear and simple:

"Be with the person across from you without speaking."

The exercise was only two minutes long, but a lot of strange behavior took place during that short period. Some people put smiles on their faces as if to say, "Hi. This is silly, isn't it?" Others stared intently into their partner's eyes, thinking that somehow, that was what had been asked of them (it wasn't.) Some people avoided eye contact and looked down. Some people tried to use hand signals. Some people looked a little nervous, others a little tense. After the two minutes were over, we explored what was going on. Most people had felt very uncomfortable, and the smiling, hand gestures, intense stares, or avoidance of eye contact represented various ploys to evade what they were feeling. The point of the exercise was not to evoke discomfort. It was an experiment designed to reveal what was truly going on within these people.

Later, there was a series of questions tracking just what had been going on, which assumptions people were making, and the cause of their discomfort, anxiety, and stress. We found that they all thought they had something to hide from their partner, and, ultimately, from themselves. A typical exchange looked like this:

Why did you smile?
To make my partner comfortable.
Why did you think she wouldn't be comfortable?
Because we weren't saying anything.
True, but why would not talking make her feel uncomfortable?
I don't know. I guess because I felt uncomfortable.
Why?
I didn't want to feel… exposed.
What didn't you want her to see?
Me. I guess… me.
What's wrong with you that you didn't want her to see it?
Nothing.
So why try to hide?
Okay. Maybe something.

If she really saw you the way you are, do you think that would be good news or bad news?

Bad news.

It feels like bad news? How bad?

Really bad?

Do you have an idea about what that would be?

There's something wrong with me.

What?

Something. I can't put my figure on it, but something not nice.

And that's what you didn't want her to see?

Yes.

So smiling wasn't to make her feel more comfortable, but to make sure she didn't see you for how you think you really are?

Yes.

As we further explored this area with the class, everyone discovered that they had trouble just being with another person. The same reaction held true as they thought about the people in their lives, yet the cause of the discomfort always tracked back to something each person felt about him- or herself: what they thought of as "bad news," something about themselves that they didn't want others (or themselves) to know about.

The next stage in this process was to have each person face whatever it was they were avoiding. Through a series of closed-eye exercises, they came in contact with the parts of themselves that they had been hesitant to see. Some people thought of it as a dark, negative, destructive aspect of themselves. Others thought of it as a character flaw—the capacity to be cruel, damaging, and harmful. This was the bad news they were trying to avoid knowing about.

Did these people have a capacity for the darker aspects of human nature? Yes—in the sense that we all do. This may come as a surprise to many people. Partly, ignorance of one's own "dark side," as we might call it, comes from social convention. In Western culture, children are supposed to be raised as if they are innocent, pure little people. In older traditions, the transformation from childhood to adulthood dealt with the acknowledgment of some darker capabilities—not so that these tendencies would be expressed in destructive acts, but so that the adult knew that he or she had a choice to act according to their higher values. Oliver Emberton, writer, entrepreneur, artist, and founder of the software company Silktide, has said,

> "Yes. In fact, humans *need* **a dark side, of sorts.** Anthropologists have identified many traits that appear universal for all humans—these appear in *every single human culture we've ever encountered.*"

Robert Bly's book *Iron Man* deals with this tradition using the Brothers Grimm tale about a wild, iron-skinned man mentoring a prince to maturity. Similar traditions from other cultures perform coming-of-age rituals in which a young person must spend time alone in the jungle, surviving whatever hardships there are. The major challenge: facing him- or herself.

Ironically, Bly's book spawned a men's movement. It could just as well have spawned a women's movement, or an anybody's movement. There is nothing terribly gender-related about the principle of Iron John that couldn't also be true for Iron Jane and the princess; yet it became another identity movement, attracting many men who needed to bolster their gender identity. City-dwelling men sat in sweat lodges as if they were Native Americans from an ancient past, hoping to define themselves better than they had done thus far. The men's movement created a synthetic ideal for men to adopt—but as with all ideals, it could only fail, in the end.

There exists a tradition that is similar-sounding, but light years away from the artificial mannerisms of the men's movement—and that is what happens during hunting season in rural places like Vermont. Fathers (and sometimes mothers) take their children to hunting lodges during hunting season. The children learn about nature, about the reason to thin out the deer population before winter (so most of them won't starve due to overpopulation) and about respect for the forest, camping, taking care of the land, and being responsible for safety. Many kids who have gone through these experiences never forget them. They are the closest thing we have to a rite-of-passage ritual in our culture, and it is very positive and wonderful.

In our Western culture, we do not have formal rites of passage. We are raised to think of ourselves as innocent of such things. The closest we come to such rite-of-passage rituals is watching horror or science fiction films. In the original *Star Wars*, Luke Skywalker must learn to overcome his foe, Darth Vader. In the *Wolfman* films, a man must fight his wolf side, which becomes dominant during the full moon. In *The Invisible Man*, a scientist invents a way to change the body's refractive index to one of air, and becomes invisible. He then becomes unhinged and destructive.

There have been countless other examples of these types of stories through the centuries. All of them give us a chance to look at ourselves from a safe distance, and from that perspective, to get to know this part of ourselves. Many of these are cautionary tales. *Look out! The moon is full. Don't hang out with vampires. Don't mess with the natural world, or you might just invent a Frankenstein monster.* Others involve glimpses of human nature disguised as a fanciful monster. One of the most classic of these tales is the *Strange Case of Dr. Jekyll and Mr. Hyde*, the novella by Robert Louis Stevenson first published in 1886. Dr. Jekyll is a good doctor who inadvertently invents a compound that turns him into a monster, Mr. Hyde. Get it? Hide?

When we tracked participants' reactions to their source, the folks in the workshop almost universally thought that they themselves were not to be fully trusted. Furthermore, they suspected their partners would see in them some type of monster that they imagined to be embedded within themselves—no matter how nice they were, or how virtuous their manners.

No wonder they couldn't be alone with themselves. They thought that the unacceptable, dark side of their nature would take them over. We don't have the kinds of ritualistic rites of passage that some cultures use to bring their youth to maturity. Western culture has had its struggles in dealing with the dark side of human nature—and the answer was to pretend it didn't exist. As human beings, we are capable of the most awful acts or the most destructive deeds. We are brainwashed into thinking that only very evil people are prone to such things—but make no mistake, we are all capable of being destructive under certain circumstances. *It is important to understand that capability is not inclination.* While we might be able to crash our car into oncoming traffic, we are not inclined to do so—and here lies the insight that shows the true temperament of most people: they want to lead good, productive lives.

Let's take a closer look at the dark side. Is it evil? Certainly, humanity is fully capable of evil acts, but just who are the people who perpetrate destructive behavior—those who are in touch with their dark side, or those who are not? From a historical perspective, the worst atrocities have mostly come from those who committed them in the name of goodness, higher values—and, too often, in the name of God. They were not aware of their dark side, nor had they come to terms with that aspect of the human condition.

In reality, the so-called dark side is actually *power*. Let's say that again. It is not dark or light. It is your built-in power. This power can be used for good or evil. It is philosophically neutral. It is like an engine. Most people are more powerful than they can ever imagine, but they don't trust themselves with power. Because of this, they disempower themselves. They do so by villainizing their own power. They think of it as the Wolfman, or Darth Vader, or Frankenstein.

Let's say the dark side is electricity rather than personal power. We could villainize electricity, the way some people did in the 18th century, when it was first explored by science. In later versions of the tale, the Frankenstein monster was brought to life with electricity (in Mary Shelley's original, it was chemistry and alchemy.) In our day and age, electricity is understood as a source of power, neither good nor evil. It can be harmful: for example, the destructive force of lightning. Or it can be very useful, for everything from lighting our houses to powering our computers. Electricity itself is simply a source of power with no agenda, policy designs, aspirations, values, hopes, dreams, intentions, or personal desires. It is exactly the same for your personal power. It is a source of energy, and it is up to you how you use it.

Let's explore what most people really want, and what their deepest values are. In light of not trusting themselves with power, they cut themselves off from their own power. Why would they do that? If they were really evil, they would exploit their own power and not care about how destructive it might be. The act of cutting themselves off from power shows their true intentions: to protect others from what they suspect they are. This points to their true values, which are good, altruistic, protective, and decent.

But this strategy comes at a cost. If you cut yourself off from your power, you become less able to create the life you want. You will fall into a pattern of being reactive or responsive to circumstances, and you will not be able to position yourself to be generative and creative. You will not be able to be truly alone with yourself. If you are not able to be alone with yourself, you cannot be together with other people, because one of you will be missing in the relationship—namely, you.

To be able to be alone, you must come to terms with your dark side, not simply as an idea, but as an experience. At first, it can seem silly, or scary, or just weird. To be able to include all of yourself in a whole person is a profound, life-changing event, one in which you truly grow up, come to full maturity, and come home to yourself.

One of the best stories that represents this principle is that of the Prodigal Son from the New Testament. The story has three characters: the father, the good son, and the prodigal son. Each character represents part of ourselves. There is the father, the source of our lives; the good son, the part of ourselves that has been true to that source; and the prodigal, the part of ourselves that has gone astray. In the story, the good son stays home and supports the father, but the other son takes his money and goes off to have a good time. He squanders his money, and, because of his choices, he is down and out. He remembers he has a home, and decides to go there. He has no expectations, no demands, no pride—nothing but his desire to be home. Once his father finds out he is coming home, he rejoices by planning a celebration for the prodigal. The "good" son, in an ironic twist, goes to the father to complain. After all, he has stayed home and worked the fields, done what his father asked of him, and remained true to his father's wishes. The father tries to explain. "I thought he was dead, but he lives. I thought he was dead…"

Imagine how the father might have felt, thinking his son was dead, but finding that he was alive; how insensitive the good son was, for not putting himself in his father's shoes; and how thrilled the father must have been to have the prodigal back home again.

There is a part of you that has been true to your source, has done all the right things, has tried to be good. There is a part of you that has gone astray, has gotten into trouble, has been out of alignment with your source. That part of you wants to come home, without expectations or demands. Ironically, it is the good son or daughter part of you that would deny the reunion. This is the holier-than-thou, sanctimonious, self-righteous aspect of human nature that is unforgiving of mistakes, that sees failure and folly as unacceptable, and will not be willing to pardon the sins of the past. It is that part of us, even more than the prodigal, that needs redemption: to let yourself come home to yourself, fully and completely.

The dark side, when understood as personal power, has had a long tradition of usefulness in the arts. Without forming a healthy relationship with it, it is hard to get to something in art that is essential: emotional truth. That is why artistic development drives artists to delve into that hidden part of themselves. Here are some of the things artists have said about this:

> If we are completely honest with ourselves, everyone has a dark side to their personalities.
> —*Isabella Rossellini*

> I think the healthy way to live is to make friends with the beast inside oneself, and that means not the beast but the shadow. The dark side of one's nature. Have

fun with it and you know, is to accept everything about ourselves.
—*Anthony Hopkins*

I think we all have a little dark side we keep under wraps.
—*Fred Savage*

There's a dark side to everything.
—*Prince*

We all have a dark side. Most of us go through life avoiding direct confrontation with that aspect of ourselves, which I call the shadow self. There's a reason why. It carries a great deal of energy.
—*Lorraine Toussaint*

We all need to look into the dark side of our nature—that's where the energy is, the passion. People are afraid of that because it holds pieces of us we're busy denying.
—*Sue Grafton*

The more we deny that we have a dark side, the more power it has over us.
—*Sheryl Lee*

I don't mind telling a dark side.
—*Clint Eastwood*

The woman's perspective is like the dark side of the moon: it always exists, but it is never exposed, at least not in my culture.
—*Ang Lee*

Alone and Together

Back to the workshop. The participants have been led in a series of exercises in which they have come to terms with their dark sides, shadows, and prodigal son or daughter. They have had a chance to unify all aspects of themselves. They have come home to themselves. Now, when they are asked to be alone with themselves, they are able to do that without any hesitation. Many of them report that the chattering in their heads has suddenly gone away, as if a radio they hadn't noticed was playing was suddenly shut off. There was a feeling of space and freedom and inner peace. They had come to a certain type of personal resolution, and felt whole, able to embrace every part of themselves. For most of them, this was the first time in their lives that they had felt such inner peace and freedom.

Now they were asked to sit across from the same partner they had before. They were asked to be alone AND together with their partner. This time, there was no strange behavior. After two minutes, we explored that experience. It was totally different from the first time they had sat together. They felt comfortable. They had a sense of themselves, as well as a sense of relationship with their partner. They experienced time differently, with a sense of being in the moment, and also a sense of timelessness. They were interested in their partner. They felt at home.

This is what it is like to be alone and together with others: a true sense of relationship, because both of you are there. This ability continued on well after the glow of the workshop was over. For most participants, it became a new orientation, a new way of life.

As in the Ideal/Belief/Reality conflict, people hold unwanted beliefs about themselves that they hide from themselves—to their own detriment. Once they become fluent in what these concepts are, there is a type of transformation, a change of underlying structure. Identity is no longer at issue. People can now focus upon their highest aspirations and deepest values as the subject of the creative processes in their lives.

The Individual within Social Structures

It is possible to be a full individual without compromise within a social structure—and, in fact, that is the best way to build a society. As Ben Franklin said, we are social animals. We need to be with others, join together on behalf of common purposes, interact, joke, gossip, and share important moments. Seeing a film in a movie theater with others is a different experience than seeing the very same film at home. One of the best things in life is to join with others in a collective creative process in which a team of people brings something into being, such as a film, a play, an orchestra, a local newspaper, or community projects—building a community of people focused upon creating optimal health and well-being, building our towns, states, and countries. In this day of social media, it is surprising how, with more connectivity, we are increasingly isolated. Teens in the same room don't talk to each other now. Instead, they text each other. Technology is a double-edged sword. It makes it easier to connect, almost instantly, but it also disconnects us with electronic walls. Yet the human need for relationship doesn't go away. It is a universal quest for love, family, friends, connection, and bonding. While many find spiritual pursuits on the individual level, to worship with others is a completely different experience.

When identity issues are no longer at play, a new world of relationship becomes possible with others—and with yourself.

You can be alone and together within a social structure, and that makes everything better.

WHAT YOU SHOULD GET OUT OF THIS CHAPTER

- People are social animals, and need to be involved with other people.
- Extreme isolation leads to harmful psychological effects.
- While people need to be with other people, they often find it hard.
- To be with others, you need to be able to be alone while together with others.
- The reason why many people find it hard to be alone is that they have not formed a relationship with their "dark side."
- Many other cultures have a rite of passage in which young people have a chance to get to know their dark side and incorporate that part of themselves into their lives.
- Western society pretends that a dark side of humanity does not exist. This leads to people not trusting themselves completely.
- When people do not trust themselves, they cut themselves off from their own creative power.
- When people come to terms with their dark side, they are able to be alone with themselves.
- Once they are alone, they can also be together with others.
- You can come home to yourself by integrating all parts of yourself. At that point, identity is no longer an issue.

Chapter 17

IDENTITY AND COACHING, CONSULTING, PSYCHOTHERAPY, AND TEACHING

IDENTITY ISSUES become more complex when there are two or more of you. The fields of coaching, consulting, psychotherapy, and teaching are particular disciplines that demand alignment about the outcome on both sides of the relationship. For example, in the martial arts, neither master nor student must have their identities involved with how well it is going. The student can't be thinking, "Look how well I'm doing," nor can he or she be thinking, "Look how poorly I'm doing." The teacher can't be thinking, "Look how well I'm teaching," or "Look how poorly I'm teaching." Both of them must shift their focus to the immediate technique or approach at hand. Within the martial arts, there is no place for self-indulgence or self-focus.

All of the Possibilities

Here are all of the possibilities for two people in a consulting/client, or teacher/student, or therapist/patient relationship:

Coach:	Identity	Outcome	Outcome	Identity
Client:	Identity	Identity	Outcome	Outcome

The worst of all worlds is if both the coach and the client make the coaching about themselves. The best of all worlds is when both of them are focused upon the desired outcome they both want to achieve. When that is the case, it is easier for the coach to point out the current state in relationship to the desired outcome—in other words, mutual *structural tension.*

In fact, in the long traditions of the arts and sports, this type of focus upon a desired outcome and current reality is the only way to enable the student or athlete to reach far beyond him- or herself and benefit from the teacher's mastery. In Humphrey Burton's superb biography of Leonard Bernstein, he writes:

> "Bernstein reminisced with Lukas Foss about their piano teacher Isabelle Vengerova and showed how Koussevitzky had taught him to conduct the space between the beats. Michael Tilson Thomas described a coaching session with Bernstein in which they made up rhymes to match the energy of the big theme in Schumann's *Rhenish* Symphony. He said he worshiped Aaron Copeland for what he taught him, 'What NOT to write, what to throw away.'"

Bernstein also said, "Teaching and learning are not the opposite of each other. They are intertwined."

The teacher/student relationship in the arts is unlike anything found in traditional education. It can be tough; the teacher does not take the time to soften the lesson. Actors who received training with the likes of Lee Strasberg or Stella Adler knew not to look for ego-strokes. They got a real assessment of their current level of skill, and a firm direction for the future. Even though their training was not a warm bath, they experienced some of the best education an actor could have. These great teachers produced some of the best actors there were/are: Marlon Brando, Robert De Niro, Harvey Keitel, Anthony Quinn, Warren Beatty, Melanie Griffith, Karl Malden, Sydney Pollack, Jane Fonda, Eva Marie Saint, Scarlett Johansson, Chris Evans, Marilyn Monroe, Montgomery Clift, Alec Baldwin, Uma Thurman, Barbra Streisand, Sally Field, Jon Voight…the list goes on and on. Talent alone is not enough in this field. Professional training enhances whatever talent an actor might have. Neither student nor teacher can waste time massaging the other's ego. Strasberg said, "An actors' tribute to me is in his work."

In sports, the coach holds the special position of enabling the team to reach for its highest, yet always telling them the truth about their current level of performance. This represents another example of structural tension, in which the entire team is holding a vision of the desired outcome, and also seeing reality for exactly what it is. Inspiration alone can never do this, and if inspiration is all that drives you, what do you do on the days you are not inspired? Olympic basketball coach Mike Kryzewski said, "I have a rule on my team: when we talk to one another, we look each other right in the eye, because I think it's tough to lie to somebody. You give respect to somebody."

The highest levels of performance in the arts and sports demand both aspiration and a clear fix on reality. In order for this level to be achieved, there can be no room for distortion, nor can there be room for taking this Herculean effort personally. In rigorous training, both sides of the relationship will feel all kinds of emotions, from intense frustration to the height of elation. The professional knows that he or she may have intense emotional experiences during extended periods of growth and development, but that is like the weather: sometimes it rains, and sometimes it's sunny, and that doesn't stop you from getting to work.

Muhammad Ali, certainly the greatest boxer in history, had a very clear strategy he used before he ever got near the ring. He would taunt his opponent with personal insults, calling them ugly, stupid, slow, brainless and so on. He didn't really think they were at all like he was describing them, but if he could get them to focus on themselves and their identity, he had the advantage. He knew it wasn't about his identity—it was about winning fights. He would drive the point home to his opponents by describing himself as beautiful and graceful, "The Greatest;" they, in contrast, were terrible, and unworthy of being in the ring with him. His strategy was to get them to become unprofessional by thinking in terms of identity.

Complexity

For those of you who help others, a complicating factor can develop due to the fact that they will often have their focus on their identity, at first. This is especially true when the coaching is about losing weight or making other lifestyle changes. You may be teaching them all the right things to do, but if their focus is on themselves, your effectiveness will be limited. So, you have at least two jobs: one is the actual coaching or training, and the other is to help them reorient themselves. This doesn't happen by accident. Usually, the coach needs to bring the situation to their attention. They need to understand just where their focus is—and what their motivation is. If they make it all about themselves, it will be hard to change and learn. If they make it about creating the desired end result, then a new world opens to them, and they can see reality for what it is, which is critical. Mutual structural tension opens up new worlds of possibilities. This becomes available when both coach and client place their focus on their mutual desired outcomes, and reality as it currently exists. What could be better?

WHAT YOU SHOULD GET OUT OF THIS CHAPTER

- In consulting, coaching, teaching, or the helping professions, identity issues can be more complex.
- The best position for everyone is to be focused on the desired outcomes rather than identity.
- Often, at first, the person on the receiving end of the support will have his or her focus on identity.
- One of the jobs of the support person is to help the client refocus upon desired outcomes.
- Mutual structural tension is the key ingredient for those in the helping professions.

Chapter 17

TWO WORLDS

LET US DESCRIBE two different types of worlds. One world has an identity obsession; in the other, identity is never an issue, and people are free to pursue their highest aspirations and live in accordance with their deepest values, without regard for how it makes them look, or how they feel about themselves.

In the "identity" world, it matters what you think about yourself, which group you belong to, how successful you are, and what others think of you. In this world, everything you do is a reflection of you. Sometimes, it is overt, like the person who has a *look-at-me* show going on all the time. For some, it is subtler. They know how to hide their obsession, even while everything they do is self-referential.

In the second world, people are able to learn without an identity crisis; they can make mistakes on the way to achieving their aspirations; they can see the missteps they have taken, and admit them freely; they are able to see others as the individuals they are, faults and all; and they can appreciate the human condition three-dimensionally.

Two different worlds, worlds apart. One world is quite natural. It comes from our earliest moments in life, seeking to know our boundaries. We begin to get a sense of ourselves as separate entities, as individuals. Ownership becomes important: "Those are MY toys!" Later, we begin to associate with certain groups: at first, our families, then our schoolmates, our peers, and our friends. Later still, we begin to think in broader terms as citizens, members of a community, members of a generation, members of a time period—and, through it all, we are searching for the right way to define ourselves: our identity.

The idea of identity is reinforced everywhere in our society, and places us into categories: class, race, religion, geography, politics, tastes in music, food choices, TV programs, the type of car we drive, the type of job we have, and so on. The world tells us that all of these classifications are important. To many in the world, they are—though not because of any intrinsic meaning held by the categories, but because of the ways they define us. What first was a good thing—developing a sense of your individual self—eventually becomes a burden as you try to find, and then live up to, some form of identity.

Yet another step in our maturation process involves a change in our focus, orientation, and underlying life structures. One action we can take is to refocus upon the outcomes we want to create rather than questions of how to define ourselves. This is not natural, but all true disciplines are unnatural. It takes a certain awareness to shift your focus from yourself to the outcomes you want to create—and it makes all the difference. As one person put it, "Now it's not like fighting the dragons and demons. It's almost comical when you can look at yourself, when you were so concerned with how you looked to others and to yourself. In relationships, you can be natural, relaxed, warts and all. And so can they. Life becomes more interesting, exciting, and involving."

This book has one central theme: *get your attention off of yourself and onto your life-building process*. When you do, your sense of well-being and involvement with the world (and your life) goes up dramatically. This should be easy, but it is not. Why? Because it takes UNLEARNING even more than it takes learning.

Learning and Unlearning

Often, in order to learn something new, you must *unlearn* something: when you fill a tub with fresh water, you have to drain the old water. That description isn't quite right, because it suggests that there only so much room in your brain, and to put more in, you have to trash some of the old files. It is more like this: the new learning may be in conflict with the ideas you've picked up along the way. Most people are better at adding new ideas and techniques than they are at unlearning what needs to be replaced.

A few years ago, it was popular for people to say with a certain pride, "I'm a lifetime learner." That was a phrase that was in vogue, and, in fact, it was a good idea—but too often, they thought of a "lifetime learner" as a collector of things, just as one might collect stamps or baseball cards or recipes. These types of collections do not lead to contradictions. To have a Babe Ruth baseball card doesn't contradict also having a Ted Williams baseball card.

You can't agree with Darwin's theory of evolution AND creationism. They say two completely different things about the origins of the species. If you thought one was true, you would have to think the other was not. New learning often contradicts old learning, and if one is truly a "lifetime learner," a lot of unlearning would come with the territory.

People don't usually talk about unlearning. You hardly ever hear someone say, "I'm a lifetime UN-learner." Yet that's what true learning might take. Robert Frost observed that there are some very educated people in the world, and of course, they will resent having to learn anything new. His observation has a built-in assumption: that these very educated people have their identities tied into how much they know. For such a person, new learning is made harder because it creates an identity crisis. Ideas cannot be considered based upon their own merits. They become abstract symbols of how smart the person is. This may represent one reason why the phrase "lifetime learner" has lost some of its popularity. Too often, the phrase itself is about identity.

The ability to change one's mind in light of new information or experience is essential to true learning. Peter Senge likes to use the word *metanoia*, an ancient Greek term that means *a change of one's mind*. The thought is so right; it is the orientation, the flexibility, the suppleness of mind in which unlearning becomes as common as learning.

But don't make unlearning a matter of identity. Keep your eye on reality, so you don't end up congratulating yourself on all the learning or unlearning you've done, returning to focus on yourself: "Look at me as I've given up my self-obsession."

Don't confuse working on yourself with developing skills, emotional resilience, steadfastness, discipline, awareness, and other necessary attributes to further develop your life-building process. Developing yourself is not about your identity, but about your life-mastery. There is nothing wrong with you the way you are right now. Your motivation for change is not to solve your life as if you were a problem, but because you have aspirations and values that guide your sense of direction.

You have two different worlds in which you can live. One is all about you and your identity; the other is about creating the life you want to live. They are worlds apart.

WHAT YOU SHOULD GET OUT OF THIS CHAPTER

- You can live in two different worlds.
- One is about your identity.
- The other is about your life-building process.
- You may need to unlearn as much as you need to learn.
- Don't make either a matter of identity.
- Two different worlds: worlds apart.

EPILOGUE

We, the authors, know this book might ruffle a few feathers in the self-help world, in that most of what we are saying contradicts very popular notions that, over the years, have been presented as almost indisputable. Through our work over a period of decades, however, we have found the self-help world to be filled with misconception, questionable practices, and well-meaning people. There is nothing wrong with wanting to improve your life. That is a very good thing. And one of the most powerful inroads to true improvement is the ability to eliminate your identity issues. Too often, self-help drives people in the wrong direction: to more and more self-focus. How well one does is taken very personally, thereby escalating identity issues.

In a way, the point of the book is very simple: get your focus off of yourself, and onto the outcomes you want to create. Some ideas take more getting used to than others, especially if you have paid a lot of money and taken a lot of time to learn the old ideas. What could motivate this change of mind? A few things: evidence, good sense, logic, experience, and one of the best confirmations you can have: a greater degree of success and accomplishment, a sense of well-being, a sense of direction, newfound energy, improved health, and what we could call "editorial" control over your own life. Of course, self-help is always promising these results. Too often, though, the results are fleeting, built into an oscillating pattern in which the first experience of progress is soon reversed, and things are back to the way they used to be.

Throughout the book, we have pointed to the principles of structural dynamics as the cause this oscillation. More importantly, we have described the structure that best supports your life-building creative process: structural tension. We want you to succeed at having more and more of the life you want to live. That doesn't happen by holding the right beliefs, or having faith in the universe—or through determination, thinking good thoughts, or even being a nice person. It comes from learning, experience over time, trial and error, missteps and mistakes, discipline, and not taking things personally, so that you are in the best position to understand your next steps in life.

The best approach to what we have described is to put it into practice: first as experiments, then as habits, and later, as a way of life. From this, new worlds can open for you. You can experience new joy and involvement, and life can move from an ongoing struggle to a true creative process. We wish you the very best.

ACKNOWLEDGMENTS

THERE ARE MANY PEOPLE who have contributed their talents, insights, wisdom, and energy to this book: Rosalind Fritz, Eve Fritz, Norma Kelsey, Neil Baird and Ivan Fritz. Also, thanks to the Structural Consultants around the world.

Thanks to Lori Andersen and the amazing team of leaders and health coaches and corporate partners that make up the community that is awakening the world to the possibilities of optimal health and wellbeing! Your openness to grow and create is the fuel that drove this book to completion!

We'd also like to express our appreciation and thank the amazing design team at Gardiner-Richardson who designed the cover and diagrams: Darren Richardson (principal), Gino Di Meo, Jennifer Westmoreland, and Emma Douglas. We are also grateful for the support of book designer Dede Cummings and copyeditor Cathryn Lykes of DCDesign Books, and everyone at SPC Print Integrated for helping us in the creation of this book. And to Marshal Carper—thanks for all your work and dedication to helping us change the world!

ABOUT THE AUTHORS

Robert Fritz

For over thirty years, Robert Fritz has been developing the field of structural dynamics through his work, first in the area of the creative process, and then in the area of organizational, business, and management issues. He is the founder of Robert Fritz, Inc., and, along with Peter Senge, Charlie Kiefer, and David Peter Stroh, co-founded of Innovation Associates.

Fritz began to lead courses in the creative process as applied to personal effectiveness in the mid-Seventies. He then trained others to lead his courses, and now over eighty thousand people have participated in these trainings throughout the world.

His first major discovery was the macrostructural pattern, which describes the long-range patterns in people's lives. While each individual's pattern was unique, he observed that there were two general types of patterns that people had in their lives: oscillating, and advancing. In the late Seventies, he began his work on two basic questions: why do these patterns exist and what does it take to change them from oscillating to resolving?

These questions led Fritz to pursue deeper questions about the structural make-up of human motivation, which eventually lead him to create the field of Structural Consulting. His first major book on the relationship of structure to human behavior was the international best seller *The Path of Least Resistance*, followed by *Creating, Corporate Tides, The Path of Least Resistance for Managers, Your Life as Art, Elements–The Writings of Robert Fritz*, and *The Managerial Moment of Truth*, co-authored by Bruce Bodaken. These books, along with his trainings have introduced revolutionary ideas about the influence of structural causality on human beings, both as individuals and within organizations.

As a consultant, Fritz has helped many organizations put the structural approach into practice, and his clients include Fortune 500 companies, many mid-size companies, as well as governmental and non-profit organizations. Working with other structural consultants, Robert Fritz, Inc. is at the forefront of revolutionary change in how organizations structure themselves to produce sustained high performance.

Fritz began the study of structure as a composition student at the Boston Conservatory. Later, he has studied on scholarship at Internationale Ferienkurse für Neue Musik Darmstadt, Germany, and was on the faculty of New England Conservatory of Music, and Berklee College.

After receiving his BM and MM in composition, Fritz worked as a studio musician in New York and Hollywood, and won positions in *Playboy* and *Downbeat* magazine readers' polls. As a composer, Fritz has won commissions from groups such as Boston's Collage-New Music and Dutch Radio. He has composed music for film, TV, and theater, as well as CD's. Two of his arrangements appear on the album *Celtic Ladies*, which topped Billboard Magazine World Music.

Fritz is also an award-winning filmmaker. He has written and directed several feature films, documentaries and dramatic shorts. He films have won over 90 awards from film festivals around the world.

Fritz lives in southern Vermont, with his wife and colleague, Rosalind.

Dr. Wayne Scott Andersen

Dr. Wayne Andersen is a visionary speaker, best selling author, and global thought leader who is shaping the health of America. He believes everyone has the power within to be the creative force in their own lives. Dr. A pioneered the emerging specialty of critics care medicine in the hope of better serving mankind. After 18 years of reacting to disease as the Director of Surgical Critical Care Program at Grandview and Chairman of the Department of Anesthesiology, he realized that it was time to start helping his patients create health. He then knew the time was right to pursue his true goal in life and took the bold leap out of hospital-based practice to dedicate his life to helping the world achieve optimal wellbeing. Dr A is the co-founder of Take Shape For Life, where he leads a team of thousands of Health Coaches and Health Professionals supporting and empowering others to reach their optimal health and wellbeing, including their spiritual, mental, emotional and physical potential.

He is a *New York Times* best-selling author of *Discover Your Optimal Health*, and his comprehensive system which includes *Dr. A's Habits of Health* and *Living a Longer Healthier Life* has sold over 500,000 copies.

He lives in Annapolis, Maryland with his wife Lori and his two daughters Savannah and Erica.

We offer a range of programs in the creative process and structural dynamics for individuals as well as for those that work within organizations. We also offer some programs that can be delivered in-house to organizations.
To learn more: www.robertfritz.com
Email: seminars@robertfritz.com

Robert Fritz's books include: *The Path of Least Resistance, Creating, Corporate Tides, The Path of Least Resistance for Managers, Your Life As Art, The Managerial Moment of Truth, Elements – The Writings of Robert Fritz*

Creator Tools, Inc.

Dr A

Dr. Wayne Scott Andersen

Dr. A believes that everyone has the potential to create optimal wellbeing in their lives, regardless of their current reality. Through his work as a physician, author, speaker, and mentor, Dr. A has helped tens of thousands of Americans transform their habits, putting them on the path to live longer, healthier lives.

He has expanded his interests to help people reach the highest version of themselves in their life building processes and create overall wellbeing.

Learn more about how Dr. A can help you get healthy at DrWayneAndersen.com or you can email him directly at info@drwayneandersen.com to learn more about the Habits of Health System and joining our optimal health community as a client, patient, or to become a health coach.

Books by Dr. A

Dr. A's Habits of Health—Combining cutting-edge medical research with common sense and gentle guidance, the bestselling Dr. A's Habits of Health is a single source for weight loss and permanent, radiant health.

*Discover Your Optimal Healt*h—Go from surviving to thriving with this New York Times bestseller! Thousands of people worldwide have started their health journey by following this easy-to-use guide.

Habits of Health Workbook—Living a Longer, Healthier Life is a critical piece of self-actualization. It's the difference between just reading about creating health and actually doing it.